WE BELIEVE

WE BELIEVE

Grace Baptist Assembly

© GRACE BAPTIST ASSEMBLY
139 Grosvenor Avenue,
London, N5 2NH,
England

Published by Grace Publications Trust
for Grace Baptist Assembly

Distributed by Evangelical Press
12 Wooler Street, Darlington,
County Durham, DL1 1RQ
England

ISBN 0 946462 00 3

The Baptist Affirmation of Faith 1966
      First published 1966
      Second editon 1973

A Guide for Church Fellowship
      First publlished 1974

This combined edition first published 1983
      Reprinted 1996

Printed by The Bath Press, Avon

WE BELIEVE

This publication comprises two historic documents which were approved by the Strict Baptist Assembly, as indicated in their respective introductions, which have been retained.

GRACE BAPTIST ASSEMBLY which has succeeded the earlier Assembly commends these documents to the churches, with the hope that they will contribute to the grounding of the Churches in the faith and will stimulate continuing reformation of life.

Contents

Part One

The Baptist Affirmation of Faith 1966

The affirmation of faith:

"In the fear of God and in the bonds of christian love, we, assembled pastors and deacons of the Strict Baptist denomination, solemnly avow our faith as set out in the Strict Baptist Affirmation of Faith, 1966, to be published in the form adopted in this assembly in London, May 21st, 1966.

These are the things most surely believed among us, which we desire to hold in christian love and to proclaim faithfully to the world, to the glory of God now and forever."

Grace Baptist Assembly, which has succeeded the Strict Baptist Assembly, also commends this Affirmation to the churches for their help and benefit.

In the interests of clarity and completeness minor additions and some rewording have been made in this second edition.

CONTENTS

THE DOCTRINE OF GOD

1

The Holy Trinity

WE BELIEVE there is one true and living God; a pure spirit without any material parts whatever; whose very essence is love; who is self-sufficient; immutable. eternal, omniscient, omnipresent, holy, almighty and incomprehensible. In all his relations outside himself he is sovereign, gracious, righteous, just, longsuffering, merciful, and approachable through Christ only.

> Deut. 6:4; Jer. 10:10; 1 Cor. 8:4; John 4:24; Deut. 4:15-16; Luke 24:39; 1 John 4:8; 2 Cor. 13:11; Isa. 48:11-12; Mal. 3:6; James 1:17; Deut. 33:27; Psa. 90:2; 1 Tim. 1:17; Isa. 40:13-14; 46: 9-10; Psa. 139:7-11; Jer. 23:24; Isa. 6:3; Rev. 4:8; Gen. 17:1; Rev. 1:8; Job 11:7; 26:14; 1 Tim. 6:14-16; Psa. 135:6; Eph. 1:11; Psa. 103:8; 111:4; Ex. 34:6; Isa. 45:21-22; John 14:6; 1 Tim. 2:5.

United in the one essence of God there are three persons, the Father, the Son and the Holy Spirit. These are separate persons since the Father is not the Son and not the Holy Spirit, and the Son is not the Holy Spirit. Each of these persons possesses the entire divine essence undivided, and therefore the perfections which belong to God belong to each of the three persons.

The Father is of none, neither begotten nor proceeding; the Son is eternally begotten of the Father; the Holy Spirit is eternally proceeding from the Father and the Son.

> Mat. 3:16-17; 28:19; 2 Cor. 13:14; 1 John 5:7; John 14:26; Psa. 90:2; John 1:14 and 18; 8:42; 16:28; 15:26.

2

God's Decree

God is love, and therefore all his counsels and actions proceed from this his essential nature.

> John 3:16; 1 John 4:7-16.

God has decreed in himself before the world began, by his most holy, wise and sovereign will, all things whatsoever that come to pass, but in such a way that he is not the author of sin; nor is violence done to the will of the creature, nor is God's use of means or second causes removed but established by the decree. God is sovereign and man is a responsible creature.

Isa. 46:9-10; Rom. 9:15; Eph. 1:11; 1 Pet. 1:16; James 1:13; Acts 2:23; 4:27-28; John 19:11; Prov. 16:33.

By this same decree, God has from eternity predestinated an innumerable multitude of persons to be conformed to the image of his Son with all the blessings of eternal life; the rest of mankind he has sovereignly left to act in their sin to their just condemnation.

Eph. 1:4 and 9 and 11; Rom. 8:29-30; 1 Pet. 1:2; 2 Thess. 2:13; Mat. 11:25-26; Rom. 9:17-24; 1 Pet. 2:8; Rom. 1:28; 2 Cor. 13:5; 2 Tim. 3:8.

The predestinated persons, the elect, were chosen by God before the world began, entirely of his own good pleasure, and not at all on account of any faith or good works foreseen in them. As God has appointed the elect, and only the elect, to glory, so has he by the same decree foreordained all the means thereto, so that the elect being fallen in Adam, are redeemed by Christ, effectually called unto faith by the Spirit, justified, adopted, sanctified, made to persevere to the end, and at length glorified.

Eph. 1:4-5; 2:8-10; Rom. 8:28-30; Phil. 1:6.

This doctrine of predestination is to be taught with reverent prudence and care, that all men may be warned to be concerned for their state as sinners; and that the elect, making their calling and election sure, may be comforted and encouraged, and built up in their holy faith, to the glory of God's sovereign majesty.

Acts 20:27; Rev. 20:15; 2 Pet. 1:5-10.

3

Creation

In the beginning it pleased God, for the display of His glory, power, wisdom and goodness, to create out of nothing the heavens and the earth, and all that is in them.

God also created the first human pair, male and female, with intelligent and immortal souls, and made after the image of God, being perfectly righteous and holy, and completely able to fulfil the law of God implanted in their nature. The description of creation in Genesis 1 and 2 is not myth but an accurate historical account of creation given by divine revelation.

Gen. 1:1-2; John 1:3; Heb. 11:3; Psa. 19:1; Rom. 1:2ᵒ; Gen. 1:27; Mat. 19:4; Gen. 9:6; James 3:9; Eccls. 7:29; Job 38 and 39; Psa. 104:24; 33:5, 6; Col. 1:16; Rom. 11:36; Isa. 43:7; Rev. 4:11

4

Divine Providence

God the Creator, in his infinite power and wisdom, sustains and governs all creatures and things by his most wise and holy providence, according to his infallible foreknowledge and unchangeable will, to the glory of his invincible and righteous purpose.

Heb. 1:3; Dan. 4:34-35; Acts 17:24-28; Mat. 10:29-30; Acts 15:18; Eph. 1:11; 3:9-10; Isa. 64:4.

Although all things come to pass with certainty according to God's foreknowledge and decree, so that nothing happens without his providence; yet by the same providence God often uses means so that things happen according to the nature of second causes, either necessarily or contingently. Though God has normally worked in accordance with the laws of nature, or through second causes, there are occasions when he has worked directly or immediately. These extra-ordinary providences, or miracles, are a display of divine power wherein God works in a supernatural way, producing a result without recourse to the normal means. The miracles of Scripture were performed with a definite purpose in view, and were especially manifest during periods of unusual revelation.

Gen. 8:22; Jer. 31:35; Acts 27:31-44; Ex. 7:1; 1 Kings 18:38; John 2:11.

This same providence, by God's almighty power and wisdom governs the actions of men and spirits, so that while they act freely according to their natures, their deeds, whether good or bad, fall within the scope of the divine purpose. This applies equally to the case of those from whom God sovereignly withholds his mercies with the result that they are hardened in their sins. Nevertheless, sinfulness comes only from creatures and not from God.

Acts 2:23; 4:27-28; 14:16; Psa. 76:10; Isa. 10:5-7.

While the providence of God governs all things, it is specially concerned with the sustaining and building up of the Church and the welfare of its members.

Psa. 23; 103; 125:2; Isa. 43:3-5; Eph. 4:11-16.

THE HOLY SCRIPTURES

WE BELIEVE that in creation God has given a revelation of his power and glory leaving all men without excuse before him, but none by the light of nature alone can attain to a saving knowledge of God. This revelation leaves all men without excuse before God. For this reason it pleased God to give by the Scriptures a written revelation of that knowledge of himself and his will necessary to salvation.

Rom. 1:18-21; 2:14, 15; Psa. 19:1; Heb. 1:1; Rom. 3:1, 2.

By the Scriptures, or Bible, we mean only the sixty-six books of the Old and New Testaments. The books known as the Apocrypha, not being inspired, form no part of the Scriptures. In the absence of the original manuscripts, God has divinely preserved his work in many faithful copies. Careful translations are to be made that all men might personally read God's Word in their own language.

Isa. 40:8; Mat. 5:18; John 5:39.

The Scriptures have their origin in God himself; they are God-breathed, given by inspiration of God. This inspiration extends to all the books in their totality, down to the very words used, and is not limited in any way whatever either by man's understanding or response. The Scriptures do not therefore merely contain God's Word, they are God's Word.

Ex. 4:10-15; 2 Sam. 23: 1-2; Jer. 1:9; 2 Tim. 3:16; 2 Pet. 1:19-21; John 17:17.

The authority of the Bible depends wholly upon God and is unique and supreme. It alone is the only sufficient, certain and infallible rule of saving knowledge, faith and obedience. Therefore the Bible is the authoritative Word of God to all people, and a sure and complete guide in all matters of christian thinking, living and service.

2 Tim. 3:15-17; 2 Pet. 1:19-21; Heb. 1:1; Rom. 15:4; Isa. 8:19, 20; Psa. 19; 119:105; 1 Cor. 2:13; 1 Thess. 2:13.

The Bible attests its own divine authority and this is not contrary to human reason, but is demonstrated by convincing evidence. This authority, however, is only experienced by faith, through the inward working of the Holy Spirit bearing witness by and with the Word in our hearts. In this way the power and teaching of the Holy Spirit in the Bible itself are made clear in the understanding, assurance, joy and eternal good of the individual believer.

1 Cor. 2: 4; 15:1-6; 1 Thess. 1:5; Luke 1:1-4; John 6:45; John 16:13, 14; 1 Cor. 2:9-14.

The Bible is its own interpreter, and so we compare Scripture with Scripture. The Bible is a unity of truth and contains no real contradictions. When, therefore, there is a question about the true meaning or full sense of any part of the Bible, it must be determined by other parts that speak more clearly.

1 Cor. 2:13; 2 Pet. 1:20-21; Acts 15:15-16.

The Bible is to be proclaimed and taught as having power in itself, through the Holy Spirit, to regenerate, convince, convert, save and keep all of God's children. God may use other means to these ends, but never without, or in a way inconsistent with, the truth of the Bible.

Heb. 4:12; 1 Pet. 1:23-25; Eph. 5:26; Acts 2:37.

In all controversial matters, whether of religion or life, the teaching of the Bible is to be taken as decisive and final. If in anything the Bible appears to be silent, we cannot allow or approve of that which is inconsistent with any clearly defined principle or teaching of the Bible.

Isa. 8:20; Mat. 22:29-31; Acts 28:23; Rom. 4:3.

THE DOCTRINE OF ANGELS

WE BELIEVE in the existence of good and evil angels. These are spirit beings possessing intelligence, will and power, though subject to the limitations which belong to creatures.

Heb. 1:7, 13, 14; Mark 13:32; Mat. 25:41; 2 Pet. 2:4.

All angels were created holy and some, maintaining their integrity, continue in a state of holiness and glory. They are employed in the worship and service of God and also to minister to God's redeemed people. The evil angels did not keep their first estate but, in opposition to God, became fallen spirits. They are commonly designated demons in Scripture.

Mat. 18:10; Rev. 5:11; Heb. 1:14; 2 Pet. 2:4; Jude 6; Mark 1:25.

Of these fallen spirits, one is clearly revealed as exalted in rank and authority over his associates. He is the Devil, or Satan, the great enemy of God and man. His power over the bodies and souls of men is very great. He is the opposer of all good and the promoter of all evil. Yet the Devil is not almighty, nor omnipresent nor omniscient. The powers of Satan and his angels are always and in all forms strictly under the sovereign control of God.

Mat. 4:1-11; John 8:44; Job 2:6; 2:7; Eph. 2:2; 6:12.

Satan and all demons can and ought to be resisted by all christians in the strength and might of Christ who was manifested to destroy the works of the Devil. Every attempt to communicate with the spirit world is forbidden in Scripture. The final appointment of the Devil at the end of the age is to everlasting torment.

James 4:7; 1 Pet. 5:8; Gen. 3:15; Ex. 22:18; Gal. 5:19-20; Rev. 20:10.

THE DOCTRINE OF MAN AND SIN

Nature, Origin and Results of Sin

WE BELIEVE that sin is disobedience to the law of God, resulting in a position of guilt and in a condition of positive evil in the nature of men. This condition is not only an absence of good or failure to do right, it is an entire distortion of human nature producing habitual rebellion against the will of God.

> 1 John 3:4; Rom. 3:19; 8:7; Col. 1:21.

Sin began, not in God, nor in man, but among the angels before the creation of man. The biblical history of the entry of sin into the world and of the fall of Adam is factual and is the foundation of basic doctrine in Scripture.

> Gen. 2:15-17; 3; Rom. 5:12-21; 2 Cor. 11:3; John 9:3; 11:4-15; Rev. 12:7-9; Isa. 14:12; Luke 10:18; Rom. 16:20.

Adam was the representative of the human race and the sentence passed on him was passed on all mankind. All Adam's posterity is without exception dead in sin, entirely defiled, guilty before God, subject to the death of the body, and deserving of eternal judgment. This explanation of man's plight is not an excuse for continuing in sin, for all are accountable to God. The body is not in itself sinful but is made the instrument of sin and the excuse for it by fallen man.

> Gen. 3; Rom. 5:12-19; 1 Cor. 15:20-25; Eph. 2:1-5; Ezek. 18:19-20.

Natural man is totally unable to receive God's truth or to desire true godliness because his mind is blinded and his heart is wholly inclined to evil.

> Mat. 16:17; Eph. 4:18.

God has given man power to choose his own course of action. His will is not forced from outside himself against his inward disposition, but always operates in

19

harmony with his own personality, emotional and intellectual state. He is thus responsible and accountable to God for his choices.

Until the fall man was able to choose either to please God or to disobey him. Since the fall man still chooses freely according to his own nature, but that nature is now sinful and dead towards God. Consequently, all his decisions, both in material and spiritual affairs, lack the enlightenment of the divine will and he is completely unable to please God, to choose Christ, or in any way to contribute to his own salvation from sin.

> Deut. 30:19; Josh. 24:15; James 1:14; Mat. 7:15-20; 15:19; Gen. 2:16-17; 3:6; John 6:65; 15:5; Rom. 8:7-8; Eph. 2:1; John 6:44; Heb. 11:6; 9:14; Isa. 64:6.

In salvation God frees the sinner from this bondage enabling him to will and to enjoy all spiritual good. Indwelling sin, however, remains to ensnare the believer; he is still liable to choose evil, or to choose good and yet fail to achieve it, until he is perfected in glory.

> John 8:36; Rom. 7:14-23; Eph. 2:5; 4:13; Gal. 5:16-17; Phil. 2:12-13; Jude 24; Eph. 6:10-18; 1 John 3:1-3; Psa. 17:15; Phil. 1:6.

THE DOCTRINE OF THE GRACE OF GOD

1

General and Special Grace

WE BELIEVE that God is gracious in his very nature. Grace is that perfection of God in which he shows unmerited and even forfeited favour in a general way to all mankind and in a special way to the elect.

> Ex. 22:27; 34:6; Neh. 9:17 and 31; Psa. 86:15; 111:4; Isa. 30:18; Jonah 4:2.

There is that grace which is general, in that God is good to all. It appears in the natural blessings which God showers upon all in this present life, in spite of the fact that man has forfeited them and is in a state of condemnation. It is seen in all that God does to restrain the devastating influence and development of sin in the world, and to maintain and enrich the natural life of mankind in general. It is entirely due to this general grace of God that human existence is possible and life bearable, useful and of value.

> Psa. 145:9; Mat. 5:45; Acts 14:17; Rom. 1:24, 26, 28; 1 Tim. 4:10.

Special grace is that which secures and brings salvation to the elect of God. This is the crowning work of God's grace and is manifest in the whole scheme of salvation and its application to the individual believer in his life here on earth and in eternal glory. Thus it is that all true christians owe everything to the grace of God.

> Rom. 3:24; 5:2 and 17-21; 1 Cor. 15:10; Eph. 1:6, 7; 2:5-8; Col. 1:6; Titus 2:11; 1 Pet. 5:10-12.

2

The Covenant of Grace

Having regard to man's helplessness as a sinner, God, being both righteous and gracious, has taken the initiative to save his people by his own act of mercy. He has done this by means of a covenant, known as the Covenant of Grace.

By this covenant God himself provides the surety in the person of the eternal Son who, by his passive and active obedience in his holy life and in his sufferings and death, merited a righteousness which is imputed to

21

the elect. By this same covenant God himself imparts new life through the Holy Spirit to those who are by nature dead in sin, and brings them to the knowledge and experience of salvation.

On the grounds of this covenant sinners are made partakers of all the blessings of the gospel being, as to their standing before God, completely freed from the guilt of sin; and as to their experience, delivered from the dominion of sin though its presence and influence are still with them.

This covenant is entirely of grace, because it is produced by a unilateral and voluntary act of God and depends only upon the divine activity of the Trinity for its fulfilment. It is also eternal, being once and for all secured to the believer by the sacrificial death of Christ, and particular because its benefits are bestowed personally and individually upon the elect.

Isa. 42:6; 49:7-8; Jer. 31:31-34; Rom. 4; Titus 1:2; Rom. 1: 1-2; Heb. 8:6-10; John 17:2, 9, 10, 24; Heb. 7:22.

3

The Person and Work of Christ the Mediator

The nature of God's covenant of grace necessitates the office of a mediator to bring about the reconciliation of sinful man with a holy God. This need, God in His wisdom and grace, has met in the person of Jesus Christ, who, truly God, became also truly man, yet without sin. He was born of the virgin Mary by the agency of the Holy Spirit whereby the two natures, divine and human, are mystically joined in one glorious person, called in the Scriptures the mediator of the new covenant.

This office the Lord Jesus willingly assumed and perfectly fulfilled. He was crucified and died, and remained in the state of the dead, yet saw no corruption. On the third day he arose from the dead, with the same body in which he suffered. Afterwards he ascended into heaven, where he sits at the right hand of the Father, and from whence he shall return to be the Judge of all at the end of the world.

Psa. 40:7, 8; Heb. 10:5-10; John 10:18; Mat. 1:23; Luke 1:35; John 1:14; Gal. 4:4; Heb. 8:6; 9:15; Acts 2:23, 24, 32, 33; 1 Cor. 15:3, 4; John 20:25-27; Mark 16:19; Acts 1:9-11; Rom. 8:34; Heb. 9:24; Acts 10:42; Rom. 14:9, 10.

The work of the Lord Jesus Christ as mediator is exercised in all phases of redemption. In him the elect were chosen before the foundation of the world, and were predestinated to be conformed to his image. By his perfect obedience and sacrifice of himself which he by the eternal Spirit offered up unto God in their stead, he has fully satisfied the justice of God, propitiated his wrath, and obtained for the elect redemption, reconciliation to God and an everlasting inheritance in the kingdom of heaven. By him they have access into the grace of God, and to God himself, and by him are assuredly called and kept.

Heb. 9:15; 1 Tim. 2:5; Eph. 1:4; Rom. 8:29; Heb. 9:14; Rom. 3:24-26; Eph. 1:7; 2 Cor. 5:18-19; 2 Pet. 1:3-11; Rom. 5:2; Eph. 2:18; John 14:6; 10:3-5 and 27-29.

As mediator the Lord Jesus Christ combines the offices of prophet, priest and king: As prophet, both before and after his incarnation, he declares to men the nature and will of God.

As the great high priest, who in his perfect humanity is touched with the feeling of the infirmities of his people, he has passed into the heavens, offering his own blood, and ever lives to make intercession for them. The thanksgiving and prayers of the elect are presented to God through him.

As king, all power is given unto him in heaven and earth; the dead, both just and unjust, will be raised at his summons, and he shall reign until he has put all enemies under his feet.

Deut. 18:15-19; 1 Pet. 1:11; John 17:8; 1:18; Heb. 4:14-16; 9:11-15; 7:25; Rom. 1:8; John 14:13-14; Mat. 28:18; John 5:26-29; 1 Cor. 15:25.

The Lord Jesus Christ is the one and only mediator whom God has appointed between himself and man, and only he, by his dual nature of God and man in one holy person, can possibly fulfil this office. Every soul that thirsts for the benefits of his mediatorial work has direct access to him without the exercise of any other intermediary, and all who thus come are assured of a gracious reception.

1 Tim. 2:5; John 7:37; 6:37.

4

The Person and Work of the Holy Spirit

The Holy Spirit is revealed in Scripture as the executor of the counsels and purposes of the Godhead. He is seen at work in the control of the material universe; in the inspiration, preservation and interpretation of the Scriptures; in relation to the Church and its witness in the world; and especially in his gracious dealings with the children of God.

The Holy Spirit is the divine agent in convicting men of sin, in the new birth and in all that follows in the christian life through saving faith, communion with God and power in prayer, and sanctification and transformation of character. It pleases God to give to believers or to churches, from time to time, unusual seasons of awakening and refreshing by the Holy Spirit.

Isa. 32:13-17; Zec. 12:10; Acts 3:19; 4:31.

It is the supreme work of the Holy Spirit to reveal the things of Christ, to guide into all truth and to glorify the Lord Jesus Christ.

Psa. 104:29, 30; 1 Pet. 1:11; Acts 1:16; 2 Tim. 3:16; John 3:5-8; 1 Cor. 2-12; Eph. 2:18; 3:5; Rom. 8:26, 27; Rom. 8: 2-4, 11; John 14:26; 15:26; 16:13-14.

5

Regeneration

Regeneration is the implanting of spiritual life of which the Holy Spirit is the source and agent. By this new birth all the elect are made, in God's appointed way and time, a new creation in Christ Jesus. There is conveyed in the new birth, in which man is entirely passive, that grace by which the sinner is enabled to receive and respond to the saving revelation of God in Christ, and without which no man can receive the things of God.

At the new birth the various graces of the Spirit such as repentance and faith are conferred, and by means of these the recipients are brought to an experience of salvation in Christ Jesus.

The new birth, effectually uniting the sinner to Christ, gives possession of eternal life.

Titus 3:5; John 3:5; 1:11-13; 3:8; Rom. 8:30; Psa. 110:3; 2 Cor. 5:17; Eph. 2:1-6; John 1:12-13; 1 Cor. 2:14; Rom. 6:17-18; John 10:27-28; 17:24; Rom. 8:14-17.

6

Effectual Calling

Those whom God has predestinated unto life he effectually calls by his Word and by the Holy Spirit, their minds being spiritually enlightened and their wills being renewed, so that, being effectually drawn to the Lord Jesus Christ and enabled by His grace, they come most willingly.

This effectual call is of God's free grace alone, not from anything foreseen in man nor from any power or agency in the creature, being dead in trespasses and sins until quickened and renewed by the Holy Spirit.

All men being dead in trespasses and sins neither can nor will truly come to Christ for salvation unless effectually drawn by the Father.

Rom. 8:30; James 1:18; 1 Pet. 1:23; 1 Cor. 1:9; 1 Thess. 1:5; Eph. 1:17-18; Ezek. 36:26; John 6:37; Psa. 110:3; Eph. 2:8; 2 Tim. 1:9; 1 Cor. 2:14; Eph. 2:1-6; John 6:44.

7

Justification

Those whom God effectually calls, he also freely justifies by pardoning their sins and by accounting and accepting them as righteous. This he does, not for anything wrought in them, or done by them, but for Christ's sake alone; not by imputing faith itself but by imputing Christ's active obedience in his life unto the whole law, and passive obedience in his death for their complete and only righteousness.

Faith, receiving and resting on Christ and His righteousness, is the sole instrument of justification.

Rom. 3:24; 8:30; 4:5-8; Eph. 1:7; 1 Cor. 1:30-31; Rom. 5:17-19; Phil. 3:8-9; Eph. 2:8-10; Rom. 3:28.

Christ by his obedience and death has fully discharged the debt of all who are justified; and did by the sacrifice of himself—undergoing in their stead the penalty due to them—make a proper, real and full satisfaction to God's justice on their behalf.

Believers, being justified, have a standing in Christ which cannot alter, yet they may, by their sins, fall under God's fatherly displeasure and so mar their state, losing the light of his countenance until sin is confessed and pardon assured through the continuing forgiveness of God.

Heb. 10:14; 1 Pet. 1:18-19; Isa. 53:5-6; Rom. 3:24-26; 1 John 4:10; John 10:28; Psa. 89:31-33; 32:5; 51; Mat. 26:75; 6:12; 1 John 1:7-9.

8

Adoption

God undertakes, in and for the sake of his Son Jesus Christ, to confer the grace of adoption on all those who are justified. In this way they are taken into the number, and enjoy the liberties and privileges, of the children of God. They have his name put upon them, receive the spirit of adoption, have access to the throne of grace with boldness, are entitled and enabled to call God, Father. They are pitied, protected, provided for, and disciplined by him as by a father, yet never cast off, but sealed to the day of redemption, and inherit the promises as heirs of everlasting salvation.

Eph. 1:5; Gal. 4:4-5; John 1:12; Rom. 8:17; 2 Cor. 6:17-18; Rev. 3:12; Rom. 8:15; Gal. 4:6; Eph. 2:18; Psa. 103:13; Prov. 14:26; 1 Pet. 5:7; Heb. 12:6; Isa. 54:8-9; Lam. 3:31; Eph. 4:30; Heb. 1:14; 6:12.

9

Sanctification

Those who are united to Christ are sanctified in him. The work of sanctification in believers is, however, carried on through Christ's Word and the Holy Spirit dwelling in them.

The effective ground of this sanctification is the blood of the covenant shed by Christ for his Church.

1 Cor. 1:2 and 30; Heb. 2:11; John 17:17; Eph. 3:16-19; 5:25-27; Heb. 9:13-14; 10:10 and 14 and 29.

Believers are commanded to be filled with the Spirit. As responsible beings they ought, through the Holy Spirit, to put to death the deeds of the body and, denying ungodliness and worldly lusts, they should live soberly, righteously, and godly in this present world; yet in this life they are never completely freed from the corruption of sin and from this corruption there arises a continual warfare between the flesh and the spirit. Nevertheless through the continual supply of strength from the sanctifying Spirit of Christ the new nature does overcome and so believers grow in grace, perfecting holiness in the fear of God, pressing after a heavenly life, in obedience to all the commands of Christ.

Rom. 8:13; Col. 3:5; Titus 2:12; Rom. 7:18 and 23; Gal. 5:17; 1 Pet. 2:11; Rom. 6:14; 7:22-25; 2 Cor. 3:18; 2 Pet. 3:18; 2 Cor. 7:1.

THE DOCTRINE OF SALVATION

1

Conversion

WE BELIEVE that conversion results from effectual calling, and is the state in which the new nature implanted
in regeneration becomes active, so that the called persons are consciously involved in salvation, and turn to
God.

Conversion always includes the vital elements of
repentance and saving faith.

Repentance:

God commands all men everywhere to repent. True
repentance is a Spirit-wrought change both of mind and
will, which brings a personal conviction of sin, a true
sorrow for it and a turning from it. This repentance is
experienced in different ways and at different times in
the lives of the children of God, and increases in depth
as the Holy Spirit reveals some fresh aspect of the cor-
ruptions of human nature.

Repentance is not necessarily and exclusively sorrow
for particular sins committed by the individual, nor is it
only remorse. It is the continuing work of the Holy Spirit
leading to Christ, creating a consciousness of the sinfulness of the heart and life, and of failure to reach God's
perfect standard.

> Acts 17:30; 1 Thess. 1:9-10; Acts 20:21; 26:16-18; Isa. 6:5;
> Luke 18:13; 2 Cor. 7:10.

Saving Faith:

Faith, whereby the children of God come to trust in
Christ to the saving of their souls, is the work of the Holy
Spirit, and is commonly brought about by the ministry
of the Word of God. Saving faith is the gracious gift of
God bestowed upon the elect only, and this faith once
given is never withdrawn, but the conscious enjoyment

of it can be clouded by sin, by doubt, or by neglect of Bible reading, christian fellowship, and the ordinances of God's house.

John 1:12; Acts 15:6-11; 16:31; Gal. 2:20; Eph. 2:8; 2 Tim. 1:12.

2

Assurance

Those who truly believe in the Lord Jesus and love him in sincerity, and who endeavour to walk in all good conscience before him, may in this life be certainly assured that they are, by grace, the children of God and are in a state of eternal blessing.

1 John 2:1-3; 3:14-24; 5:13; Rom. 5:2 and 5; 8:14-16; Heb. 10:22.

This certainty is clearly taught in the Scriptures and is based upon an understanding of the saving work of Christ, wherein the believer trusts; and it is further confirmed by the inward witness of the Holy Spirit. It results in humility and a desire for holiness and fills the heart of the believer with deep joy and peace, and gives sacred purpose to his life and expectation of the life to come.

Rom. 8:1 and 31-32; 1 John 3:1-3.

Normally faith in Christ, as including trust, carries with it a sense of security, but this is not experienced to the same degree by every believer. The believer may also displease God and grieve the Holy Spirit, and so the comfort of assurance may be impaired.

The development of assurance is brought about by the Holy Spirit as the fruit of reflection and growth in grace. It is, therefore, the duty of the believer to give all diligence to make his calling and election sure, so that he may live humbly and happily as one of God's children.

Mat. 6:30; Psa. 42:1-5; 73:1-17; Eph. 4:30; 2 Cor. 3:18; 2 Pet. 3:18; 1:10; 2 Cor. 6:14-18.

Perseverance

Those whom God has regenerated and effectually called into the blessings of his grace can neither totally nor finally fall away, but they shall be graciously preserved throughout life here on earth and be eternally saved.

John 10:28-29; 2 Tim. 2:19.

This blessing of the eternal security of every true believer is based upon God's purpose and power, and not upon the free will and good works of the believer. It might equally be termed "the preservation of the saints", and may be defined as that continuous operation of the Holy Spirit in the believer, by which the work of divine grace that is begun in the heart, is continued and brought to completion. It is because God never forsakes his work that believers endure to the end, yet the believer is to work out his own salvation with fear and trembling, remembering that the Lord has said: "he that endureth to the end shall be saved".

Rom. 8:28-30 and 38-39; 5:8-10; Phil. 1:6; Heb. 6:17-18; 1 Pet. 1:3-5; Phil. 2:11-13; Mat. 10:22.

THE DOCTRINE OF THE CHURCH

1

The Nature of the Church

WE BELIEVE that the Universal Church is the innumerable company of God's elect in every age, who have been, are, or will be called out of the power of Satan to God, regenerated by the Holy Spirit, and redeemed from sin through the blood of Christ. This Church will endure to the end, and will be complete and perfect in the day of Christ.

Mat. 16:18; John 17:24; Eph. 3:14-15; Acts 2:47; 26:18; Eph. 5:25-27; Phil. 1:6; Col. 1:12-14; Heb. 12:23; Rev. 7:9-17.

It is the duty of all believers, walking in the fear of the Lord, to unite with local churches, for their own sanctification, and the maintenance of gospel witness.

Such churches, having the presence of Christ as head, are responsible to him for their own administration, and in this respect are independent of every other form of control, whether of Church or State. They have the fulness of God, and to them is committed the stewardship of the Gospel, the defence of the truth, the discipline of disorderly members, the appointment of officers, and the administration of the ordinances.

Mat. 18:15-20; Eph. 1:22-23; Acts 13:1-4; 1 Cor. 5; 2 Thess. 3:6; 1 John 4:1; Rev. 2 and 3.

Christ is the appointed head of the church, his authority never being delegated to men, but communicated to the church by his Holy Spirit. The church seeks, not merely to discover the opinion of the majority of the members, but rather through prayer and fellowship to know the mind of the Lord.

Mat. 28:18-20; Col. 1:18; Eph. 1:22-23; Acts 2:1-4 and 41-47; 13:1-4; 15:28-31; 1 Cor. 5:4-5; Eph. 4:8-13.

The Church of Christ has been put in trust with the Gospel of the grace of God, and it is its solemn responsibility to go into all the world and proclaim that Gospel to every creature.

Mat. 28:19, 20; Mark 16:15; 1 Thess. 2:4.

2

The Local Church and its Worship

The church is maintained and increased as the Lord adds to its number those who are being saved. The local church should be composed of those who are subjects of divine grace, exhibit the fruit of the Spirit, and hold the apostles' doctrine.

Acts 2:47; Rom. 14:1; 1 Thess. 1:5-6.

We believe that all men should serve and fear God, but that true worship, springing from the hearts of the redeemed, must be with understanding, reverence, humility, faith, love and submission, through Christ the only mediator, and by the Spirit, to the Father. It is the duty of the church to provide for the united worship of the Lord's people in praise, prayer, edification and the proclamation of the Gospel in the locality of the church, in the country and throughout the world. Failure to fulfil these duties brings the Lord's displeasure, but obedience is encouraged by the promise of the Lord's presence and blessing.

Ex. 20:4-6; Psa. 95:1-7; Jer. 10:7; Mark 12:33; Mat. 4:9-10; John 4:23-24; 14:6; Rom. 8:26; 1 Cor. 14:15-17; Eph. 2:18; 4:15-16; 5:19; Col. 3:16; 1 Tim. 2:1-5; 4:13; 2 Tim. 4:2; Mat. 28:19-20; Rev. 2:5.

3

The Ordinances

We recognise two ordinances, so called because ordained or established by Christ's authority, namely Baptism and the Lord's Supper.

These ordinances are to be administered by those appointed by the church, and are to continue until the end of the world.

Mat. 28:19; 1 Cor. 11:23-26.

Baptism

The ordinance of Baptism is to be administered in the name of the Father, and of the Son, and of the Holy Ghost. The candidates in this ordinance express their separation from the world, and their identity with Christ in his death, burial and resurrection, and their devotion henceforth to him.

The ordinance is to be administered only to those who have exhibited repentance for sin and made a profession of their faith in Christ.

The ordinance is rightly administered by the total immersion of the candidate in water, this mode alone being scriptural and having reference to the burial and resurrection of Christ.

This ordinance is essential, not to salvation, but for obedience to the commandments of Christ, and for a full and complete profession of faith.

Rom. 6:4-6; Acts 22:16; Rom. 6:5; Col. 2:12; Acts 2:38; Gal. 3:27; Acts 2:41; Mat. 3:15, 16; Acts 8:38-39; Rom. 6:4; Mat. 28:19-20; Mark 16:16; Acts 10:44-48.

The Lord's Supper

The ordinance of the Lord's Supper is regularly to be observed as a memorial of the sufferings and death of Christ, and an expression of the inherent unity of the Church as one body in Christ, and as a means of strengthening the faith of the believer. It is in no sense a sacrifice, nor the continuation of the sacrifice of Calvary.

The administration of the ordinance involves the sharing of bread and wine, both of which are to be received by the communicants, and are symbols of the body and blood of Christ. At no time during the course of the administration, or because of the administration, does any change of nature take place in the bread or in the wine, which the communicants are themselves to take and to eat or drink.

This ordinance is a means of grace through the spiritual presence of Christ, apprehended by faith in the heart of the believer. Those worthily taking part feed upon Christ crucified and all the benefits of his death; the body and blood of Christ being spiritually present to the faith of the believer, as the elements themselves are to the outward senses.

Those who partake unworthily sin against Christ and are guilty of offence against the body and blood of the Lord, eating and drinking judgment to themselves.

We believe the administration of this ordinance is to be restricted to baptised believers in the New Testament sense of those words, and such restriction is signified by the term "Strict Communion". Each local church applies this principle as it deems right and con-sistent in its administration of the Lord's Supper.

1 Cor. 11:26; Heb. 10:12; 1 Cor. 11:27-30 and 23-25; Luke 22:19-20; Mat. 26:26-27; 1 Cor. 10:16; 11:29; Acts 2:41-46; Compare Acts 18:8 with 1 Cor. 10:16-17.

The Responsibilities of Church Members

Members of churches are required first to give themselves to the Lord and then to one another by the will of God. They are not to forsake the assembling of the church for public worship, fellowship in prayer and the Lord's Table, but are to seek the spiritual prosperity of other members, and to provide for the material relief of needy members. Members are also required to support and to contribute regularly and sacrificially to the Lord's work at home and overseas through the funds of the church.

Acts 11:29-30; 1 Cor. 12; 16:1-2; 2 Cor. 8:1-5; Eph. 4:28; 1 Thess. 5:14; Gal. 6:10; Heb. 3:12-13; 10:24-25; 1 John 3:17-18.

5

Church Officers and their Appointment

We believe that the ascended Lord bestows gifts upon men for the maintenance of his work on earth, and that the administration of local churches is to be by elders and deacons. Among the elders are those whom we call pastors, and these are set apart for prayer and the study of the Word, and should, so far as is possible, be adequately maintained in material necessities, so as to be disentangled from the cares of a secular calling.

Elders are responsible for the spiritual ministrations of the church, watching over the souls of the members as those who must give account. It is the duty of the members to support their elders by prayer, and to submit to their admonitions in the Lord.

Deacons are responsible for the business and secular affairs of the church, which are to be administered with spiritual grace.

Acts 20:17; Phil. 1:1; Eph. 4:7-12; 1 Tim. 3:1-13; Heb. 13:17; 1 Cor. 9:6-14; Gal. 6:6-7; 1 Tim. 5:17-18.

The appointment of elders (including pastors) and deacons, for office within the local church, and of preachers and missionaries for the work of evangelism is the responsibility of the local church under the guidance of the Holy Spirit. The Lord's ordination is recognised both by the experience of the inward conviction, and by the approval of the church observing the possession of those gifts and graces required by Scripture for the office concerned. The one so called should be set apart by the prayer of the whole church.

Acts 6:3-6; 14:23; 1 Tim. 4:14; 1 Pet. 4:10-11; 1 Tim. 3:1-13; Acts 13:1-4.

6
The Discipline of the Local Church

Believers are admitted through baptism into all the privileges of the local church and also into its discipline, being bound by prayer and endeavour to maintain unity and peace. Members who persist in denial of fundamental doctrine or who, by their ungodly conduct, bring dishonour on the church ought to be disciplined. In matters of personal offence members should first seek reconciliation with one another privately, if this fails the elders of the church should be consulted, and if need be the matter should be submitted to the judgment of the church itself. Believers should not take brothers in Christ to the civil law, nor should they disturb the peace of the church over personal disputes.

All discipline in the church should be exercised with love and patience, as well as in accordance with the teaching and examples of the Word, and the end in view must always be the repentance and reconciliation of the offender, and the purity and blessing of the church.

Mat. 18:15-20; 2 Cor. 2:1-11; Eph. 4:2-3; 1 Cor. 6:1-7; 1 Thess. 5:14; 2 Thess. 3:6-15; Acts 2:41; 9:18-25; Gal. 6:1, 2.

7
Inter-Church Relationships

Churches, likeminded in biblical faith and practice, have a responsibility to manifest their oneness in Christ in mutual fellowship and conference.

Acts 15:1-31; Rom. 15:26; 2 Cor. 6:14-16; 8 and 9; 1 Cor. 16:1-3.

We believe that the division of the professing Church on earth into sections results largely from the departure of many from the truth of the Gospel, and in part from differences of biblical interpretation, temperament and culture. Those who are born again are bound together in an unbreakable spiritual unity in Christ.

Schisms arising from tradition and prejudice grieve the Holy Spirit and are not to be tolerated. Visible unity is desirable, but cannot be achieved by amalgamation of denominations, by joining true believers with those who are unregenerate, or by any means that compromises the evangelical faith.

Mat. 15:1-9; John 10:16; 17:20-23; Acts 15:36-41; 20:29-30; 1 Cor. 3:1-4; 2 Cor. 2:17; 11:1-5; Eph. 4:1-16 and 19-22; 2 Tim. 3:1-5.

THE DOCTRINE OF THE CHRISTIAN LIFE

1

The Law of God

WE BELIEVE that God has placed Adam and all his descendants under his holy law. By this law man is required both to love the Lord his God with all his heart, soul, mind and strength and to love his neighbour as himself.

Following the fall, God elaborated these two principles in ten commandments setting out man's duty towards God and towards his fellows.

Rom. 2:13-15; Mark 12:28-31; Ex. 20:1-17.

This law is binding upon the saved and the unsaved alike, but the motive of its observance by the christian will be love to Christ who has redeemed him from its curse.

Rom. 13:8-10; Gal. 2:20.

The christian is not justified by keeping the law, but he strives to do so because it comes to him with the authority of God, whom he loves; the man who dies unsaved is condemned by it. Its requirements are essentially spiritual, and no fallen man can fully comply with the law's demands. No such man can therefore by endeavouring to keep the law save his own soul.

One man alone, the Lord Jesus Christ, has fulfilled every requirement of the law. This he has done in his own person in the place of his people.

James 2:8-12; Mat. 5:17-19; Rom. 3:31; 7:14; Gal. 2:16; Rom. 10:4; Gal. 3:13.

Among the purposes of the law are these:

(a) To restrain the unregenerate from sin and to show what the consequences of their sin must be.

(b) To convince the sinner of the true nature of sin and of his inability to resist it by keeping the law; to strip him of all self-confidence and condemn him, so compelling him to look to the Lord Jesus Christ as the only way of escape from his predicament.

(*c*) To show the believer the will of God and his duty to his fellows; also to remind him that, although he has been saved by grace, he still has to contend with a most sinful nature, and therefore daily needs both the aid of the Lord Jesus Christ and the perfection of his obedience.

Rom. 3:20; 7:7; Gal. 3:10-12 and 23-24; Rom. 7:14-25; 8:1-4; Heb. 4:14; James 2:10, 11; 1 John 1:7-10.

It is one of the functions of the Holy Spirit to make the believer able and willing to do that which the law of God requires of him.

In Old Testament times God placed the people of Israel under a ceremonial law which pointed forward to Christ; this ceremonial law, however, ceased to have effect at his coming.

Ezek. 36:25-27; Phil. 2:13; Heb. 10:1-10.

2

The Lord's Day

We believe that God has set apart one day in seven and its observance is binding upon all men. It is to be kept holy and is designed also for man's benefit. The Church has a warrant to observe the first day of the week as the Lord's Day, because it is the day of our Lord's resurrection. No detailed instructions are given in Scripture as to the way in which this day is to be kept, but ample allowance is made for works of mercy and necessity. The day is to be used for rest from secular labour and worldly recreation, and for the occupation of the whole person in the worship and service of the Lord.

Ex. 20:8-11; Luke 4:16; Acts 20:7; 1 Cor. 16:1-2; Rev. 1:10.

3

Christian Behaviour

We believe the Scriptures teach that the christian faith is to be seen in its practical outworking between the believer and his fellow men. His words and deeds are to demonstrate the reality of his new life. He is justified by faith, and that faith will be seen in his works.

Christian behaviour is the maturing of the fruit of the

Spirit as the believer learns more of the ways of God and man. The New Testament requires that due regard be given in public ministry to the exposition of the Gospel. In all his behaviour the christian will be motivated by the glory and fear of God and by loving obedience to the rule of Christ.

The believer's relationships to governments and men in general and to his fellow christians in particular are to manifest the Spirit of Christ. In his relationship with unbelievers the christian is to set an example of life and character in every respect even at the cost of personal suffering, thus glorifying God and both rebuking and instructing the ungodly.

James 2:14-26; John 15:1-8; 1 Tim. 2; Rom. 13:1-7; 1 Pet. 2:13-25; Phil. 2:1-16.

4

The Christian Attitude to Material Things

Wealth and all material things justly obtained are to be received as God's gracious gifts, and to be used for worthy ends with a due sense of responsibility and stewardship.

For this reason and because of a deep desire to be just in all his dealings, the true christian should renounce all forms of gambling, the root of which is covetousness.

Gen. 1:29, 30; 1 Chron. 29:13, 14; James 1:17; Luke 12:15, 31; Matt. 25:14, 15; Matt. 7:12.

5

The Christian and the State

We believe that rulers are ordained by God for the orderly conduct of affairs in the world and the good of his Church, and that to this end he sets up rulers and removes them as it pleases him.

It is the duty of christians to obey those who have the rule over them in all matters consistent with the teaching of the Bible and to seek to live quiet, peaceable and honest lives. Christians are under an obligation to pray for their rulers.

A christian may properly accept public office both in central and local government and play his part in the affairs of the nation in so far as such service may be consistent with his christian profession.

Rom. 13:1-7; 1 Tim. 2:1-4; Titus 3:1; 1 Pet. 2:13-17.

6

The Christian and his Work

We believe that all men physically able to do so are under an obligation to work to support themselves and their families and to give to those in need. That everyone whatever his sphere of responsibility is to perform his daily tasks in accordance with the Scripture "whatsoever thy hand findeth to do, do it with thy might".

We further believe that relationships between staff and management are to be governed by the principles set out in the New Testament. Employees are to work conscientiously and honestly and employers are to be just and fair with their staff, both in the sight of God.

Gen. 3:19; 2 Thess. 3:10-12; Eph. 4:28; 6:5-9; Col. 3:22-25; 4:1; Titus 2:9-10; 1 Pet. 2:18; 2 Cor. 6:14-17.

7

Marriage and Family Life

We believe that marriage is a union between one man and one woman to the exclusion of all others, sealed by vows which make it life-long.

Marriage within the prohibited degrees as laid down in the Bible is forbidden.

God instituted the marriage relationship for the mutual help and comfort of husband and wife, the procreation of children and the prevention of immorality.

The sexual relationship is sacred and is not to be indulged promiscuously but only within the bonds of marriage. Sexual intercourse outside marriage, whether in contemplation of marriage or otherwise, is forbidden by the Bible, and is sin.

Christians should only marry believers and should seek to teach their children similar standards.

In all relationships the christian should exercise forgiveness and strive for reconciliation. Divorce otherwise than upon the ground of adultery is contrary to the teaching of the Bible.

We further believe that it is the duty and privilege of christian parents to rear their children in a disciplined and loving way; to see that their children acquire a thorough knowledge of the Bible from an early age and so to live that by their faith and example the true nature of the christian religion may become apparent to their children; and that children are to obey their parents in the same spirit.

Gen. 2:24; Mat. 19:5-6; Gen. 2:18; 19:1-28; Lev. 18:6-22; 20:14; Deut. 23:17; Acts 15:29; 1 Cor. 6:13-20; Gal. 5:19; Col. 3:5; 1 Thess. 4:3; 1 Cor. 7:2 and 9 and 39; Heb. 13:4; 2 Cor. 6:14; Mat. 19:9; Eph. 6:1-4; Prov. 22:6; 23:13-14; 29:15-17; Col. 3:20-21; 2 Tim. 3:15.

All forms of sexual perversion are forbidden by the Scriptures, and there is for the believer complete deliverance from these things through the power of Christ.

Lev. 18:3, 20-23, Rom. 1:26, 27; 1 Cor. 5:1-9.

THE DOCTRINE OF THINGS TO COME

1

The State of Man after Death

We believe that the bodies of men after death return to their natural elements but their souls, being immortal, immediately return to God who gave them.

The souls of believers go immediately upon the death of the body to be with the Lord Jesus Christ in glory, where they wait for the redemption of their bodies. The souls of the unsaved are reserved in hell to the day of the last Judgment. Holy Scripture knows of no such place as Purgatory or of any intermediate state.

Gen. 3:19; Eccles. 12:7; 2 Cor. 5:1-8; 2 Pet. 2:9; Luke 23:43; Rom. 8:23; Luke 16:23.

2

The Resurrection

At a time known only to God, the Lord Jesus Christ shall return to this earth in glory, bringing with Him the souls of the believers who have died. At this time the bodies of those believers who are still alive on earth shall be transformed instantaneously and without death into a condition of glorious incorruptibility, conformable to Christ's own glorious body.

The bodies of those believers who have died shall rise in like glorified condition and be reunited with their souls. All believers shall then, in their glorified bodies, be caught up to meet the Lord in the air, and so be with Him for ever. The bodies of the unsaved shall also be raised by the power of Christ.

1 Thess. 4:14-17; 1 Cor. 15:51-53; Acts 24:14-15; John 5:28-29; Phil. 3:20-21.

3

The Last Judgment

God has appointed a day wherein he will judge the world in righteousness by Jesus Christ. All mankind, being resurrected from the dead, shall stand before him and he shall separate his redeemed people from the ungodly. The earth as it is at present shall be no more, and the redeemed shall take their place, glorified in Christ's likeness, in the new heaven and the new earth, where God himself shall be with them and be their God for all eternity. The unsaved, who know not God and do not obey the Gospel of Jesus Christ, will be punished with everlasting destruction from the presence of the Lord. Thus will be seen the glory of God's mercy in the eternal salvation of all believers, and the glory of God's righteous judgment in the condemnation of the ungodly.

Acts 17:31; Mat. 25:31-32; 2 Pet. 3:10-11; Rev. 21:1-3; 1 Cor. 15:47-49; 1 John 3:2; 2 Thess. 1:6-10; 1 Pet. 1:3-5; 1 Thess. 4:16-18.

4

The Lord's Return

We believe in the personal return of the Lord Jesus Christ to this earth. The precise time of his coming again and of the day of judgment is not revealed, in order that, in the long suffering of God, men may come to repentance and ever seek to be prepared.

All true believers in times of adversity find consolation in the prospect of their Lord's return, be it sooner or later, and the whole Church of Christ may ever pray: "Lord Jesus, come quickly!"

Mark 13:32; 2 Pet. 3:9-10; 1 Thess. 4:16-18; Rev. 22:20.

Part Two

A Guide for Church Fellowship

In commending this volume to the churches, the National Assembly of Strict Baptists do so for their help and guidance. No authority is claimed for the contents other than that which inheres by divine inspiration in the scripture explicitly quoted in the material presented.

Grace Baptist Assembly, which has succeeded the Strict Baptist Assembly, also commends this Guide to the churches for their help and benefit.

CONTENTS

Part 3   WITNESS

INTRODUCTION

This guide is issued for the use of churches which are in agreement with the **1966 Affirmation of Faith,** entitled *We Believe.* It was considered desirable for the following reasons:

The **Affirmation** was prepared as a contemporary Particular Baptist Confession to promote the interests of truth and unity among those of like-mind. It was hoped that this would result, under God, not only in closer mutual appreciation of the Doctrines of Grace, but also in closer agreement in the area of practice. This guide seeks to further that end, not by fostering a mere mechanical uniformity as such, but a considered agreement arising from a careful and prayerful study of Scripture. For God's Word is our primary source of instruction.

Much material on the subject of church order and practice has appeared from Particular Baptist sources in the past, but it is not now easily accessible to churches. This book is an endeavour to fill the gap and provide a summary of the wisdom of the past and a new appreciation of our own tradition and of the work of the Holy Spirit among us in more recent study.

We suspect that the requirements and pressures of the pastoral office are not appreciated by the christian public as they ought to be. There is a need of increased understanding and spiritual insight so that the work of the ministry may be better supported and encouraged. It is further hoped that the ministers themselves will be moved, through this guide, to a more zealous and faithful discharge of the duties given to them by the great Head of the church.

As *Dogmatic Theology* may be said to pertain to the *being* of the church, so *Practical Theology* relates to the *well-being* of the church. It is therefore our belief that this guide, although by no means exhaustive, can contribute to the effectiveness and spiritual well-being of our churches.

This guide is presented by the National Strict Baptist Assembly to the churches as worthy of serious study and use. It is divided into three sections:—

1. **Worship**—the church's response to the God of glory and grace.

2. **Discipline**—the ordering of the life of the churches according to the biblical pattern.

3. **Witness**—the responsibility of the churches in the world.

These three sections are titled Part 1, Part 2 and Part 3. The Contents table gives a schedule of the subjects dealt with in the sub-division of each part.

Part 1   WORSHIP

THE WORSHIP OF GOD IN PUBLIC

Worship is adoration, reverence and praise offered to God as the blessed and holy Trinity, who is worthy of all honour and glory. It is offered in response to the glorious excellence of the very being and acts of God—what he is and what he does. The highest activity of which man is capable is ascribing to God the glory due to his name. Worship will also involve confession of sin, supplication and a sense of human obligation and dependence upon God. In it we recognise his attributes and saving acts declaring them with adoration.

Worship is divinely commanded and is therefore a sacred duty. By virtue of God's total and absolute perfection it is eminently reasonable. God **ought** to be praised. It is also a gracious privilege which we should embrace with delight and engage in with our whole being.

The christian worshipper is dependent upon the mediation of the Lord Jesus Christ and the aid of the Holy Spirit so that God may be served in spirit and in truth. Further, God has promised his gracious presence to those that meet in his name. We believe that such spiritual worship glorifies and delights him. In consequence, such worship exercises great influence on the spiritual life of the individual and the church and even on the moral consciousness of the community.

Worship should be offered privately by individuals and families. On the Lord's day, and at other times, there is also the need for what we call *Public Worship.* The individual should prepare himself for this by his own private devotion.

Truth is essential to worship. Therefore, we can not view worship as a matter of doctrinal indifference; nor can we take the precepts of human reason, feeling or tradition as our guide.

In summary, public worship should be: solemn, not light, flippant or trivial; simple, not pompous, ritualistic or ceremonial; cheerful, not gloomy or forbidding; not hypocritical but sincere and pure. Such worship is costly, but rich in blessing, pointing to the eternal occupation and happiness of the saints in glory. Consequently, avoidable lateness at a service is not only a disturbance to the minister and worshipping people, but an offence to God.

Mat. 4:10; Heb. 7:25 ff.; 1 John 2:1; Rom. 8:26, 27; John 4:24; Mat. 18:10; Mat. 5:13; John 4:23, 24; Psa. 89:7; Isa. 66:2; Psa. 100:4; Isa. 1:12; Mat. 23:13; Isa. 57:15.

THE READING OF SCRIPTURE

The canonical scriptures of the Old and New Testament are basic to christianity as the divine revelation. As such they are at the heart of the worship of God.

God speaks to men through the scriptures as they are read and preached. As God alone is the object of worship, so he alone should determine the character of our response to him through his own Word.

Because the *faith once delivered* is founded upon the whole Bible, both Testaments should be used for reading. A balanced scheme for covering the whole Bible should be aimed at, although some passages may be considered less suitable for public reading than others due to their obscurity. The actual choice of readings, such matters as whether passages from both Testaments should be read at each service and how long a reading should be, should be left to the discretion of the minister. It seems to us that the excellencies of the *Authorised Version* recommend its continued use.

The scriptures should be read in public prayerfully and in a manner becoming their character as God's Word. The reading should be taken with reverence and dignity. The reader should desire that he himself may feel the power of the Word and that the hearers may feel the same.

Due regard should be given to the exact meaning so that the true sense may be conveyed to, and understood by, all who hear. Sincerity of heart, concentration of mind and singleness of purpose will help to produce clear expression.

Neh. 8:8.

Every one should be encouraged to have his own Bible, to read it privately and to follow the scriptures read during the service.

THE PREACHING OF THE GOSPEL

Preaching has a unique place in God's plan for the salvation of his elect people. Not only must the Scriptures be read but the Gospel must be proclaimed.

The Preacher: All christians are called upon to witness to the Gospel but God grants special gifts to men whom he has chosen for public preaching. These he sovereignly sets apart and anoints by his Holy Spirit. The preacher, with these God-given qualifications, must also discipline his whole life. None are exposed to such peculiar trials and temptations nor more subject to Satan's onslaughts. The preacher must also be an example to the people, a watchman warning them against error and danger, and a shepherd caring for his flock.

Acts 13:2; 1 Peter 5:1-11; Ezekiel 34.

The Nature of Preaching: Preaching involves an orderly exposition and application of scripture. It must aim at the glory of God, in declaring both the just judgement of unbelievers and the gracious, full salvation of God's people. It should be directed at the whole man—his understanding, will and affections. It is the most powerful means of grace which he himself has ordained.

2 Cor. 2: 14-16.

The Content of Preaching: A faithful proclamation of the whole counsel of God as revealed in the scriptures has a three-fold aim:—

1. To warn men of the requirements of God's law, of their lost condition outside of Christ, of the uselessness of morality as a ground of hope and of the wrath of God upon unbelievers now and for ever. Such preaching is intended to awaken the conscience of the hearer and cause serious enquiry;

    Tit. 3:5; James 2:10; Rom. 3:20; 2 Thess. 1:7-9; Jude 15.

2. To call men to repentance and faith, pointing them to Christ alone for salvation, exhorting them to respond to the invitations of the Gospel and encouraging anxious enquirers to embrace the promise of full provision for them in Christ. Such preaching encourages sinners to call upon the name of the Lord that they may be saved;

    Mat. 11:28, 29; John 6:35; Acts 3:19; 17:30, 31; Rom. 10:13; Heb. 7:25.

3. To minister to the spiritual welfare of believers by reproof, exhortation, instruction and comfort. Such preaching leads the believer to give diligence to make his calling and election sure.

    2 Tim. 3:15; 2 Peter 1:10.

Preaching must be balanced in exposition, doctrine, experience and practice. It should be expressed in language which is simple, clear and contemporary but never crude or unseemly.

The Manner of Preaching: This vital ministry demands solemnity with joy, control with urgency, faithfulness with love, boldness with humility. This authoritative ministry arises from confidence in the message itself together with certainty that God will glorify himself through its declaration and a reliance upon the power of the Holy Spirit.

    Isa. 55:11; 1 Cor. 1:4.

The Manner of Hearing: Just as the preacher is required to be faithful in the exercise of his ministry, so the congregation are solemnly accountable for their hearing of the Word. They must give heed to the Word: first, by believing, disciplined attention and personal application, and then by the practice of the message. If they neglect this privilege and means of grace, they will be accountable for it on the Day of Judgement.

Heb. 4:2; Mark 4:24; Acts 17:10, 11; Heb. 10:25; James 1:22-24; 1 John 4:1.

PUBLIC PRAYER

The earliest recorded description of worship is to *call on the name of the Lord.* God has appointed prayer for salvation, edification, comfort and spiritual growth. Its importance cannot be overstressed on the one hand nor too carefully examined and exercised on the other. As preaching is God's voice to the people, so prayer is the people's voice to God. Both need the same unction of the Spirit and require equal care, thought and preparation.

Gen. 4:26.

Subject Matter in Public Prayer: Public prayer includes invocation, adoration, confession, petition, dedication, thanksgiving and blessing. It should be as specific as propriety allows and reflect an understanding of the needs of the people and of the world. There are certain subjects for which we are to pray constantly, such as, the glory of God, the furtherance of the Gospel, the extension of Christ's kingdom, the conversion of sinners; for magistrates, our rulers and nation, all peoples of the earth, peace in the world; for the second coming of the Lord; for our own children and youth generally, all in special want, distress, sorrow and temptation, and for the final perseverance of the saints; for the overthrow of error and evil, and for temporal and spiritual blessings. In all our

55

prayers we are to be submissive to the will of the Lord.

1 Tim. 2:1-4; Ph. 4:6; Eph. 6:18; John 12:28; 14:13; 1 John 5:14; Rev. 22:20.

Language and Address in Prayer: Reverence and sobriety (which is not to say sombreness) must be evident in our public prayer. This is vitally important because we are finite, sinful creatures addressing the infinite, holy Creator. Our language should be plain, simple, clear and becoming. We are rightly to address God as *Our Father* but must remember that our Lord taught us to follow this with *Hallowed be thy name*. The minister must remember that his congregation will include a great variety of age, experience and circumstance, and that all should be embraced within the scope of public prayer. He should take care to avoid stereotyped phrases, clichés and undue length.

Mat. 6:5-15.

Forms in Public Prayer: Historically, set forms have not been used by Free Churchmen. This is still largely the case and free prayer is our usage. However, set forms should not be wholly condemned lest we deny the example which our Lord has given us in scripture, for it appears that he gave a pattern of prayer to his disciples when, as young believers, they asked to be taught.

Luke 11:1-4.

PRAISE IN PUBLIC WORSHIP

Praise is the homage rendered to God by his creatures, in worship of his Person and thanksgiving for his blessings. It is wrong to withhold that glory which is his rightful due, for he has said *Whoso offereth praise glorifieth me*.

Every believer who meditates upon God's works, recounts his benefits, and dwells by faith upon his unspeakable gift, will find praise not only a duty but also a delight. Praise sanctifies all aspects of life. Whatever else its burden may be, prayer should be praiseful, always including thanksgiving. The Holy Spirit's grace is essential to the offering of spiritual praise.

Psa. 50:23; 11-14; 103:2; 2 Cor. 9:15; 1 Tim. 4:5; 1 Cor. 10:30, 31; 1 Thess. 5:16-18; Phil. 4:6.

The context of christian praise should be regulated by scriptural examples and principles. In Colossians 3:16 we find reference to three apparently different types of composition used in praise. These have been defined as follows:—

Psalms—spiritual poems set to music, including the Old Testament psalms, but not limited to them.

Hymns—songs of praise to the Lord. Again they may be Old Testament psalms or hymns of praise composed by christians.

Spiritual songs—compositions on distinctly christian themes, suitable to fellowship meetings of the church, sung accompanied or unaccompanied.

Matt. 26:30; 1 Cor. 14:26.

Each of these is appropriate to christian praise today. Words, tunes and accompaniments (if any) ought to be worthy of the holiness and majesty of God. The content must be sound doctrinally, the form of high quality. The music should assist praise by stimulating spiritually rather than carnally, leaving the mind to concentrate unencumbered on the words. Whatever form is used, a spirit and attitude of reverence is required. This will be reflected in a suitable tempo of singing, neither so slow as to be laboured and lethargic, nor so quick as to lack a sense of the dignity and grandeur of holy things.

Preparation for both public praise and public prayer should be made in our private devotions. We are to rejoice in the Lord always. Such praise animates the dull and soothes the agitated spirit. It comforts and inspires the saints, and attracts the unconverted more than any other part of christian worship. Christianity has sung its triumphs through the ages and around the world.

THE OFFERING

The word *offering* carries with its implications of *sacrifice*. It indicates that it has cost the donor something. The Lord's Day offering may be said to be a symbolic offering of ourselves to God. It is also an expression of our gratitude to him for what he is and for his many mercies. The offering is to him and for his kingdom world-wide. This concept of the offering holds true by whatever method the offering is set aside. This may be by viewing it as a constituent part of public worship where the giving and receiving are both seen as acts of worship in themselves, or alternatively where the offering is disassociated from the immediate acts of public worship. The motivation of faith and love and a desire to glorify God in the offering are required for it to be acceptable to God. Its giving should be with cheerfulness.

2 Cor. 8:5; 2 Cor. 9:7; Rom. 12:1.

THE BENEDICTION

It is our delight and privilege to bless God as we worship him. This is so because he has first blessed us with grace, mercy and peace in his dear Son. The biblical concept of God's blessing upon his people as they worship him is called the Benediction. It is a declaration that those who are Christ's sheep are the *blessed of his Father*. The Benediction includes supplication for the Lord's blessing, and a declaration that God's favour or his *Name* is upon his people. This does not mean that the minister imparts grace but identifies himself with the congregation by using the form *be with us*. Further, this declaration is not a *magic formula* but should be viewed as an appeal to the hearers to appropriate its contents by faith.

58

The Benediction is usually given in a Trinitarian formula, and forms the conclusion of a service.

Num. 6:22-27; Mark 10:16; Luke 24:50; Mat. 25:34.

SPECIAL SERVICES

It is right for churches to set aside special seasons for praise, thanksgiving, prayer and confession, and for the ministry of the Word. Such occasions may be specially convened in connection with some particular blessing in the life of the church, or may be regularly observed. They may be related to the history of the church or the pastorate, to some new evidence of the Lord's grace, or to a deeply felt need of humbling before God. It should always be ensured that the occasion is not merely routine, that its full meaning is understood by all, and that its primary aim is not the raising of funds or any such object, but the glorifying of God.

THANKSGIVING FOR A CHILD

Children born to christian parents have providential blessings which others do not have. They have the advantage of christian instruction, godly example, family worship and that loving care and discipline which is the fruit of the gospel. This does not mean that they are necessarily *elect* and will certainly become christians in later days. They still need, like all others, the sovereign regenerating work of the Holy Spirit leading to personal repentance and faith, if they are to be the children of God.

We have no direct New Testament command to present our children in public worship, although we have the example of Christ blessing infants. Where the children of believers are presented before the Lord in a service, the act will be regulated by the following considerations:—

1. Thanksgiving is being offered for the life given to the child, and the life spared to the mother. God's goodness in all respects is always to be acknowledged.

2. The parents are acknowledging their responsibility before God, solemnly committing themselves to it in the presence of the Lord and his gathered people, and seeking divine help for their task.

3. The gathered church is recognising its part in the life of the family, pledging itself to prayer and encouragement and praying for the child that the Lord will add to those blessings already given, those special favours designed for his own.

   Mark 10:13-16; Luke 2:28.

CHURCH CALENDAR SERVICES

The minister will not limit his preaching on the subjects of the Incarnation, Crucifixion, Resurrection and Ascension of our Lord Jesus Christ, the Trinity or the outpouring of the Holy Spirit to a few set occasions in the year. Where the regular course of the ministry declares the whole counsel of God, the centralities of the faith will be ever prominent, and special emphasis will be less necessary. Yet in a materialistic world, a clear statement of the christian position in respect of these matters is constantly needed, so that the use of those special opportunities, which custom provides, may be justified.

Part 2   DISCIPLINE

RECOGNITION OF A LOCAL CHURCH

A local church is the company of christian believers gathered together in one particular place by the work of God. It is properly distinguished by a membership which

1. is committed to a clear affirmation of sound biblical doctrine;

> Acts 2:42; 1 Tim. 4:6, 7, 13, 16; 6:20; 2 Tim. 1:13.

2. consists of those who have confessed, by believer's baptism, their faith in Jesus Christ as their own Lord and Saviour and are living a godly life;

> Acts 2:38; 10:47, 48; Gal. 3:27; Acts 18:8 cf. 1 Cor. 1:2.

3. is given, each to the other, in fellowship, prayer, worship, mutual service and evangelism;

> 2 Cor. 8:5; 1 Thess. 1:2, 3, 7-9; Acts 2:42.

4. is provided, under God, with an eldership to regulate and maintain the ministry of the Word, the regular observance of the ordinances, and the exercise of a biblical discipline.

> 1 Tim. 3:1-7, 15; 5:17; Titus 1:5-9.

Without these distinguishing marks, a group of believers does not form a properly constituted church. Such a company, lacking these features, ought to seek the guidance and ministry of the eldership of a neighbouring church.

For the sake of peace and unity among the churches, it is desirable that a newly constituted church should be recognised by the other fellowships. Where the new church arises from outreach work, it will be recognised also by the church from whose outreach it has sprung.

MEMBERSHIP OF THE LOCAL CHURCH

Scripture clearly supports the view that believers should be identified with an organised local assembly of christians.

The Nature of a New Testament Church

A readiness to accept the biblical doctrine of the Church will inevitably include acceptance of the principle of church membership. The use of the word *church* in the New Testament indicates that the early christians were not only incorporated into the One Body of Christ (the Universal Church) but also joined themselves to a local assembly (the local church). Compare 1 Cor. 12:13 with 2 Cor. 8:4. Here they covenanted together in a bond of fellowship with other believers, thus entering a particular visible society with a distinct and restricted membership. Scripture gives no grounds for a believer belonging to the Universal Church while abstaining from local church membership.

2 Cor. 8:4; Acts 2:41 ff.; 8:1; 11:26.

The Need for Organisation within a local church

The New Testament makes clear that the apostolic churches were organised. They dealt with matters of discipline, and appointed church officers. The words of Acts 6:3—*look you out from among you seven men of honest report*—presuppose that the original Jerusalem church was an organised body of converted people. The apostolic churches were disciplined, organised bodies with clearly defined memberships.

1 Tim. 3:15; Titus 1:5; 1 Cor. 14:33, 40; Mat. 18:15-20; Acts 6:1-6; 13:1-4; 1 Cor. 5:1, 2.

QUALIFICATIONS FOR CHURCH MEMBERSHIP

Evidence of regenerating grace is the fundamental condition of membership in the local church. Both the Acts and the Epistles give clear testimony to the fact that the New Testament churches were composed of believers who had submitted to Christ as

Lord and Saviour. We do not seek infallibly to discern the sincerity of anyone's profession of faith, yet the purity of the local church must be maintained by the insistence that a credible confession of Christ, evidenced by repentance and faith and declared in believer's baptism, is the condition of entry into the privileges of church fellowship.

Acts 2:41-47; 8:9-24; 16:13-15, 23-40.

We believe that an applicant for membership shall be required to give an oral testimony to his or her saving conversion to Christ, initially to those having the spiritual oversight, and then, if they are satisfied, to the gathered church. While no text commands this practice as a condition of membership, many scriptures exhort and encourage us to make known publicly the Lord's dealings with us and our faith in him.

Acts 8:36-39; Psa. 66:16; 119:74; Rom. 10:10; 1 Tim. 6:12; 1 Pet. 3:15.

As saving faith involves knowledge of what God has revealed to be believed, it should also be ascertained that the applicant can assent to the Articles of Faith of the church, understands and will be submissive to the church's discipline. While an applicant may be admitted as a member if there is not as clear insight into the Articles of Faith as may be desired, yet the applicant may not be admitted if found in any way opposed to them. It should also be ascertained that the applicant is held in good reputation.

PRIVILEGES AND RESPONSIBILITIES OF CHURCH MEMBERSHIP

The elders in their pastoral care ought to ensure that none joins the church lightly or unaware of their sacred privileges and responsibilities. Members ought to consider themselves bound by the laws of Christ and by their mutual covenant together, in his holy Name to love one another and to be faithful towards each other in word and deed. The members will enjoy spiritual joys and growth in grace will be seen in the responsible discharge of certain obligations, which include:—

The Promotion of true Christian Fellowship

The New Testament shows us the church as a company of believers bound to one another in Christ, and pledged to seek together the advancement of spiritual life, and the spread of the Kingdom of our Lord Jesus Christ. When a believer joins a church, then his responsibility is to promote such fellowship. Membership involves giving ourselves to one another. We are to hide each other's faults, bear each other's burdens, uphold each other in prayer. When church membership is seen in these terms of fellowship, it will cease to appear forbidding and will be seen rather as something delightful and desirable for every child of God.

> Rom. 12:5; 1 Cor. 10; 12:25-27; Phil. 1:27; Acts 2:42-47; 4:32-35.

Regular Attendance at the Gatherings of the Church

Clearly, fellowship is not possible apart from regular meetings together. Church members are under obligation to gather together for worship as far as is possible. Consequently, those who move from the district are not in a position to fulfil the duties of membership. Such persons should be encouraged to join another New Testament local church, where they are able to be actively involved in fellowship. Churches should arrange their meetings so that it is possible for all to meet together on some occasions.

> Heb. 10:24-25.

Financial Support of the Church

The work of the church requires finance. The scriptures indicate that members have a responsibility to contribute regularly to the support of the ministry and the maintenance of the witness as a whole. Where membership is taken seriously, money will be freely given by members under the glad con-

64

straint of a knowledge of biblical principles and a love of the Lord and his work.

2 Cor. 9:7; 1 Cor. 16:2; Luke 12:16-21; 1 Cor. 9:14.

Sharing in Decision-making

Church members should be prayerfully involved directly or indirectly in every decision of the church including the setting apart of elders and deacons, the sending out of missionaries and the practice of discipline.

Acts 1:23-26; 6:3-5; 13:1-3; 1 Cor. 5:4, 5, 13; 2 Cor. 2:6, 7; 2 Thess. 3:6, 14, 15.

Women in the Church

Scripture clearly teaches the headship of man and relates this to the place of women in the church (1 Cor. 11:1-16; 14:34, 35; 1 Tim. 2:11-15). This headship is based on man's prior creation and woman's prior fall into sin. From 1 Cor. 14:34; 1 Tim. 2:11, 12; Eph. 5:21-24 we learn that women are to take a place of submission which excludes the possibility of their ruling in the church. At the same time, women have an important scriptural function in the life of the church. Abundant evidence is provided by the passages cited below, in the first five of which the reference is not to wives but to women working alongside the elders and deacons. It is clear that the gifts of women are to be recognised and used, and that those with special qualifications are to be brought actively and officially into co-operation with the elders.

Acts 2:17, 18; 18:1, 2; Rom. 16:1-12; Phil. 4:2, 3; 1 Tim. 3:11; Titus 2:3.

Cessation of Membership

There are three ways in which membership of a Gospel church can be terminated:— by dismissal, by exclusion or by death. Personal resignation from a church is a mistaken concept. The Church is Christ's own institution—indeed, his Body on earth —and its proper dignity requires each local church to proceed on the principle that the individual cannot withdraw from the Body, but the Body must, if necessary, cut off the individual. While office may be resigned, membership cannot. A member may be dismissed by means of a letter of commendation and dismissal from his church, so that he may unite with another local church provided that his motives are proper. Exclusion is the church's exercise of its lawful authority and discipline, by which it withdraws fellowship from a person proved to be an unworthy member. His connection with the the body is dissolved, and therefore ceases. Death severs the bond of local church membership, and transfers the believer from the church on earth to that above.

Members who cannot be traced because of removal should be deleted from the church roll automatically without discussion or comment, as a matter of church business. The church roll should be regularly revised so as to represent faithfully the living fellowship of the church.

2 Cor. 3:1; 1 Cor. 5:13.

THE PASTORAL MINISTRY

The Authority of Christ

A believer's every need is met in the person and work of Jesus Christ, the only mediator. He is prophet, priest and king to his people. He is the great shepherd of the sheep. He alone is the head of the church. From him all authority in the church is derived and exercised. The whole church, elders, deacons and members should submit to his rule, through the scriptures. The Holy Spirit leads the church in a way that is consistent with the Word, of which he himself is the author. That Word shows us that the church's obedience to Christ includes submission to the pastors and other elders.

Col. 1:18; 1 Thess. 5:12, 13; 1 Tim. 5:17; Heb. 13:17.

The Appointment of Elders, including Pastors

A congregation without any elder falls short of the requirement of scripture. Where an eldership does already exist, however, it is their responsibility to bring others whom the Lord has gifted for this work before the church for their whole-hearted approval and appointment. Such men must conform to the standards laid down for an elder in 1 Tim. 3 to a significant degree. These are formidable requirements, but the gifts of Christ and His enabling grace will be found in the men of his choice. These qualifications will always be accompanied by a permanent, personal relationship and walk with the Lord, fervent love to God and the souls of men, and a zeal for the truth and glory of God. The church will solemnly set apart those on whom the Lord has bestowed fitness for the work. This setting-apart should be preceded by self-examination, repentance, prayer and an attention to the Scriptures. It is to be noted, from the Acts and Epistles, that the early church appointed elders from their own local community, which they would serve. Furthermore the churches set apart those in their own fellowship whom God was calling to serve in other spheres.

Acts 14:23; Titus 1:5; Acts 13:1, 2.

In a congregation where no eldership exists it is right and proper for the fellowship to watch for God's guidance to make suitable appointments as his gifts to particular men become apparent. In some situations it would be in accordance with biblical principles for the gathered membership to seek the help and counsel of a nearby church.

The Work of Elders

Elders are to lead the church in a scriptural order and discipline. Their work includes the pastoral care of the membership, as under-shepherds to the Lord. They are not to rule the church with arrogance but to serve it with humility, love, tenderness and impartiality. They are to ensure that all ministries in the fellowship are performed according to scripture (e.g.

1 Pet. 5:1, 2, etc.). This includes gathering for worship, the regular ministry of the Word and the administration of the ordinances, visitation of the sick, instruction of the young, and the work of evangelism. Suitable women may be appointed to assist in specific duties in association with the work of the elders.

1 Tim. 3:11; Titus 2:3-5.

Elders Gifted to Preach

Every church should realise its need of an adequate teaching ministry. The Lord equips some elders with the gift of expounding and proclaiming the Word for the purpose of edification, and these are frequently referred to as *pastors* or *ministers*. Such men must not only possess an ability to speak with authority, but an inward constraint of the Holy Spirit, giving them a sense of responsibility and obligation to preach the Gospel. They must have an unshakable conviction that this is the will of God for them. Intellectual ability and knowledge of the truth must be accompanied by a *fire in the bones* and a solemn sense of the high calling of God. Only this inward constraint will ensure a willingness to bear the sacrifices involved in this ministry. Such men may either be set apart for full-time ministry or, where this is not possible, occupied in a secular calling. These pastors may either be called from the eldership within their own church or, since the gifts of God are for the benefit of all the churches, from other local churches. In either case they should be, or become, members of the church in which they minister.

Acts 4:20; 1 Cor. 9:16; Jer. 20:9; Acts 14:23; Titus 1:5.

Training for the Ministry

Spiritual leadership in the churches demands a spiritual, educated and competent ministry. If this is lacking, there is the danger of a situation where the blind are leading the blind, to the destruction of both. The pastor has a personal responsibility to be a workman that needs not to be ashamed. He is to strive to be an able minister of the New Testament. He will endeavour to ensure that God is glorified by the best possible development and use of those faculties and abilities which he has bestowed upon him.

2 Tim. 2:15; 2 Cor. 3:6; Acts 18:26.

A pastor should continually seek competence in the various branches of theology and exegesis and in related subjects. He will give himself to these studies wholly and unreservedly, seeking some competence in the original tongues, if possible.

All pastors are called to be teachers. Some are exceptionally gifted and excel in exposition and theological understanding. The churches that enjoy the ministry of such men should realise their special obligation to make them available to all. One way of doing this is in the use of such men in training courses arranged by the churches. Where a man is set apart for full-time study to prepare himself for the ministry of the Word, the church should take great care in the selection of the course (and college, if appropriate) to which he commits himself, bearing in mind the particular gifts and needs of the man concerned.

Every church should aim at providing adequate training for those whom the Holy Spirit is calling, either by itself or in fellowship with other like-minded churches. The existence of such regular training facilities will enable churches to fulfil their responsibilities toward not only pastors but also Sunday School teachers, Youth Leaders, etc.

Calling a Pastor

When a church is seeking the Lord's guidance as to one who should regularly minister the Word to them, and particularly considering calling a man from another church, experience confirms the wisdom of the following advice:—

69

1. All necessary enquiries ought to be made by the elders. Detailed discussion of a man's personal life in open church-meeting is unseemly and ought to be refused.

2. Undue haste and undue slowness must be avoided, for the sake both of the churches and individuals concerned.

3. Any man to be considered for appointment should have the gifts and qualifications of an elder. He ought to have a good report from his own church, having been set aside by them for the ministry of the Word. None will know the use God made of him and his maturity and soundness in the faith better than his own fellowship.

4. It is desirable that only one man should be brought before the church for their consideration at a time. A deepening impression of the suitability of a certain man will be given to the church by the Holy Spirit. The elders will seek to lead the church to whole-hearted approval of the call.

5. Where possible, it is desirable that a man should serve the church on a number of occasions for some time before calling him. In every case there should be adequate opportunities for the church to meet informally with the man and, if he is married, with his wife, in the varied settings of the church life. The man and wife should be at one in commitment to the work of Christ. A minister's wife who is spiritually minded, and of a gracious disposition will be a great blessing to the church.

6. The call of God will be accepted both by the church and the minister in humble dependence upon the Lord. The call may well be accompanied by a sense of reticence and reluctance, only to be overcome by the fire of God kindled in the soul of the minister.

The Termination of a Pastorate

Scripture makes no direct provision for the termination of a ministry, except in cases requiring discipline. The following principles would seem to be in harmony with scripture.

1. The cessation of any sense of blessing upon the Word, or a feeling that another man would better take up the work, might be signs that a pastorate should be concluded. These are not necessarily conclusive evidence, for it may be that the Lord is speaking to the church as a whole, and not to the minister only.

2. A relationship of love and confidence must be established between the elders of a church, so that unavoidable irritations and disputes can be dealt with in a spirit of grace and humility.

3. If a problem arises requiring the discipline of a pastor, *i.e.* a charge of immorality or heresy, it is often wiser to bring in a trusted friend and pastor from another church to help deal with the matter. A strong eldership, however, ought to be able to take firm action in a spiritual manner.

4. If there is a problem of incompatibility, or some other obstacle to a harmonious ministry, the matter ought to be dealt with in love, humility and mutual respect. It is a reproach for any church and pastor to part, save in the bonds of love.

5. Pastors ought not to be obliged to continue in the full responsibility of their office after their mental and physical powers have abated. Elders should be sensible to the needs of an ageing pastor, and take steps to relieve him of an appropriate part of his burdens. Old age alone is not a reason for a man ceasing to minister the Word, but it is grievous to see a church decline because they have failed to supplement his work with the energies of those who are younger. Where there is a plurality of elders, this matter is more easily dealt with. It is desirable that churches give careful

consideration to proper provision for their pastors in retirement.

The Care of the Pastor

The work of a pastor in his study, the conduct of services and ministry of the Word, visitation and the care of the flock, together with daily cares, stresses and strains, take great toll of his physical and nervous energy. Indeed, these things often bring him to the point of exhaustion. Sometimes a pastor will become seriously ill, and when this occurs, the other elders and office-bearers should pastor him. He needs to be assured that his material support will be forthcoming during his time of illness, and that he has the love and prayers of his people. At such times, special provision may be necessary for him and his family. Moreover, scripture indicates that it may be possible to prevent such illnesses in the first place. Care should be taken to ensure that the pastor is supported and the burden of responsibility is shared. Proper provision for him should be made in terms of financial support, books, transport, holidays and opportunities to take advantage of refresher and training courses and conferences, where possible. Every effort should be made to enable the pastor to give his undivided attention to prayer, the ministry of the Word and the care of the flock.

Phil. 2:25-30; Ex. 18:13-27.

THE DEACONS AND THE SERVICE OF THE CHURCH

The Church a Caring Community

The spiritual vitality of the early church was evident not only in its gospel ministry but also in its whole manner of life as a serving community. The members of the churches served one another in spiritual exhortation and admonition. This mutual ministry was focused in the apostles and elders as the *servants* of the churches. This outflowing of spiritual life in mutual service may be equally discerned in the way the early churches sought to meet the material needs of their poorer members or of those undergoing persecution. The whole atmosphere of the churches was one of practical concern for those in need. There can be no doubt that this stemmed directly from the Lord himself, who declared that he did not come to be served but to serve. It was the direct and immediate effect of the outpouring of the Holy Spirit, and all the members were involved whether male or female. In manifesting this concern they recognised the members of the *household of faith* as their first priority, but believed it right to do good to all men. All this carries implications for our own day. In a society where the state accepts responsibility for the relief of the poorer citizens, the churches ought to be mindful of those in under-developed countries, and of the victims of such calamities as earthquakes or floods. It is also important to remember that a ministry of mercy need not be confined to financial aid. The relief of worry, loneliness and confusion is a pressing need in every situation and in every generation.

Mat. 20:28; Acts 2 and 4; 1 Cor. 12; 2 Cor. 8 and 9; Gal. 6:10.

The Office of Deacons

Whilst all the members of the church are to care for one another, the New Testament particularly focuses this aspect of service on a body of deacons, whose duty it is to ensure that this ministry is fulfilled in the church. The qualifications required for this office are no less spiritual than those required of elders. They are to have the *wisdom* required for handling people and money efficiently and graciously. Suitable women may be appointed to assist in specific duties in association with their work. The deacons should care for all the business aspects of church administration, since this requires the exercise of the same talents and gifts as the task of supplying the needs of poorer members.

Acts 6; Phil. 1:1; 1 Tim. 3; Acts 6:3; Rom. 16:1.

73

The Appointment of Deacons

All such service must be seen to be honest before God and before men. In the appointment of deacons in the early church no provision appears to have been made for retirement or regular elections, although 1 Tim. 3:10 may indicate a probationary period. There is the possible exception of those subject to some disciplinary action. In the contemporary situation the fixing of a term of service with a view to retirement or re-election after a number of years may be helpful in overcoming the problem of making way for new appointments. Care must be exercised so that the mechanical application of this method does not introduce a carnal approach to the solemn nature of *setting apart* those whom God has called to this work and given to the church. Similarly, care will be taken to ensure that those appointed have not merely a *fresh approach* but the spiritual maturity, as well as the administrative ability, to show that the Lord has equipped them for this work. If the Lord has given to a church more of such men than the normal ministry of deacons demands, then it may well be that he is directing the church to exercise these gifts in some other way, perhaps in an expansion of the work or the help of weaker churches. As with elders, it would seem advisable to retain the encouragement and counsel of older brethren whilst not stifling the energies of younger men. This could be ensured by an agreement to relieve older men of some of their responsibilities without requiring them to lay down their office.

CHURCH FINANCE

All our possessions as believers are the Lord's, given to us to be used for his glory. The giving of a proportion of our goods as an act of worship is our acknowledgement of this. Christian churches are required to make financial provision for the support of gospel witness and for charitable ministry to the poor. These needs may be met in two ways: (i) by regular systematic giving (*e.g.* the principle involved in Old Testament tithes); and (ii) occasional special giving as acts of gratitude or to meet a particular need. The New Testament principle is that each should set aside a portion of his goods for the Lord in proportion as He has prospered him.

1 Cor. 16:2.

The Treasurer

The treasurer will normally be a deacon and not one set apart for the ministry of the Word. He should be chosen from the membership both for his spiritual qualities and for his ability to handle financial matters. He should always remember that he is the servant of the church and not its financial director. It is his duty to keep the church informed of its financial state and to give advice to the best of his ability. Nor must he allow his concern with finance to become an end in itself. The church should have a sound financial policy but not aim at large reserves. Everything must be seen to be honest and it is proper therefore that full accounts be kept and regularly presented to the church, including those of auxiliaries within the church such as Sunday School, Women's Fellowship, etc. Every collection should, as a matter of wisdom, be counted and checked by others before the treasurer leaves the premises. It is to be desired that contributions to missions and charities from all departments of the church should be sent together by the treasurer so that the total giving of the church to such causes will readily appear in the church accounts.

Financial Responsibility

Elders set apart for the ministry of the Word should, so far as is possible, be maintained adequately in their material needs by the church and thus disentangled from the cares of a secular calling. In practice it is desirable that pastors should live at a level that represents the average of those among whom they work. Stipends should be paid regularly and promptly and be subject to annual review.

Churches should face responsibilities relating to the retirement of ministers such as adequate superannuation arrangements. They should also be alert to the financial requirements of evangelism (see page 49) and of charitable responsibilities (see page 55). Visiting preachers should receive an adequate remuneration, bearing in mind all costs of travel and pulpit supply.

The church must ensure that its property is maintained in good repair and adequately insured. The minimum risks to be covered are: fire, burglary, storm damage, voluntary-workers, public and employers' liability, as required by law. Care must be taken about the church's legal obligations towards pastors and employees, including national insurance and income tax requirements. Where there is a caretaker or chapel cleaner, the church ought to ensure that extra remuneration is made for the additional work caused by such special occasions as weddings, funerals, etc.

Members, appointed to represent the church at inter-church gatherings and special committees, should have their expenses met by the church. This applies equally to any work done for the church which involves travel, postages or equipment. Members who do not need such repayment should nevertheless accept it, out of thoughtfulness for those who are not able to bear their own expenses, even though they return it privately.

THE ORDINANCES

Introduction

By *Ordinances* we mean those outward rites which the Lord Jesus Christ has appointed to be administered in his church as visible signs of the saving truths of the gospel until his Coming again. They are *signs* in that they visibly declare the death and resurrection of the Lord Jesus Christ as the only ground of the participants' reconciliation to God, a reconciliation effected prior to his taking part in the ordinances. They are rightly described as a special means of grace—but do not constitute a means of special grace! They are specific commands of the Lord to his church and there is great reward in obedience to them. These ordinances are two in number, namely Baptism and the Lord's Supper, and they are to continue until the end of the age. Their outward elements retain their natural substance throughout. There is no saving power inherent in the water of baptism nor any organic change in the bread and wine at the supper. The two ordinances are of equal importance and it is contrary to scripture to give one more prominence than the other. Their meaning determines their necessary order. Baptism is set at the commencement of the life of faith and discipleship, and is at once a confession of and testimony to this new life begun. The Lord's Supper follows, as the continuing memorial of the source of the new life entered into by the disciple. To reverse the order of these ordinances removes much of their significance.

THE ORDINANCE OF BAPTISM

The Meaning of Baptism

Baptism is to be administered once only to each believer as an initial identification with Christ in his death and resurrection. This ordinance is the outward and visible sign of the inward and spiritual grace confessed. The outward sign speaks of the participant's identity with Christ in his dying and rising again. The confession sets forth his death to sin, and new life to righteousness by faith in Jesus Christ. Baptism is not essential to salvation, but it is vital to proper discipleship.

> Mat. 28:19; Mark 16:16; Rom. 6:3-5; Col. 2:11, 12; 1 Pet. 3:21; Gal. 2:19, 20.

The Person to be Baptised

The person to be baptised is to be, as far as can be discerned, regenerate as evidenced in true repentance and faith in the Lord Jesus Christ for salvation. In his baptism, he is avowing his submission to Christ as Lord. Verbal testimony is not sufficient. Such a testimony needs to be confirmed by the visible evidence of a work of the Holy Spirit in a hunger for the Word of God, a conviction of need of Jesus Christ, and a desire to be baptised as a believer in obedience to him. No confession by proxy or promise of a later faith on a candidate's behalf can make a baptism valid, but only his own spiritual state as a regenerate person, confessing and obeying Christ for himself.

Acts 8:27-40; Mat. 28:19; Mark 16:16; Acts 8:12; 9:18; 16:30-34.

The Manner of Baptism

Scriptural baptism is the immersion of the whole body in water. The Lord Jesus Christ himself gave example of this both in His own baptism and the practice of his disciples. Furthermore, immersion alone gives adequate meaning to Romans 6 where baptism is spoken of as a *burial with him in death* and the apostle adds *like as Christ was raised . . . so we . . .* Meticulous adherence to total immersion is not in itself a special source of grace but is a more complete setting forth of the spiritual significance of the ordinance. The primary meaning of the words employed throughout the New Testament is immersion, and they were so understood by the early church. Any inadequacy on the part of the administrator does not in itself invalidate the baptism of a proper candidate who rightly submits to it.

Col. 2:11; Mark 1:5-9; Luke 11:38; John 3:23; Acts 8:38, 39; Rom. 6:4; Col. 2:12.

Re-baptism

The New Testament church did not re-baptise. Provided that the first baptism is a valid ordinance in that the scriptural requirements are fulfilled, no further baptism is called for, either on account of a change of church or denomination or because of backsliding and restoration. As said above, defective administration does not invalidate the baptism of a proper person, so that such defects as an unspiritual baptiser or failure to immerse fully do not disqualify a candidate's baptism, provided that they are not willingly and knowingly accepted by him. Where *baptism* has been invalid, however, submission to the ordinance is not a re-baptism. Each case of a possible *invalid* baptism must be considered in the light of all the circumstances.

The Administrator

The ordinance would normally be administered by an elder, but another member of the local church may be set apart for this purpose. The spiritual significance lies mainly in the confession made by a proper candidate, and consequently it can be administered by one obedient disciple to another in exceptional circumstances. Such might be pioneer evangelism, or persecution of the church.

1 Cor. 1:14-17; Acts 8:26-40; 9:18.

The Preparation of the Candidate

In the context of normal, stable church conditions, the elders should ensure the proper preparation of the candidate, giving him a clear understanding of the step which he is taking. Care should be taken to explain the manner of administration so that all anxiety is removed. A gracious, gentle examination of his profession of faith will be made, and the spiritual meaning of the ordinance and the principles of committed discipleship within the local church taught. Church membership should normally begin with baptism. Where possible it is desirable that the steps towards it (as detailed on page 14) should be carried through concurrently with preparation for baptism, to avoid delay. Any unnecessary delay provides the enemy of souls with opportunity to distress the weak in faith. For female candidates, the use of spiritually mature women in the fellowship is commended. A candidate's youth shall not in itself be an impediment to believer's baptism, but due regard should be paid to the scriptural injunction to *honour parents* as well as to the other that *we ought to obey God rather than men*. In practice, any such conflict of loyalty frequently resolves itself, in the patience and prayerfulness of all concerned, and through the consistent, godly life of the believer. Care should be taken by both the young believer and the elders to ensure that parents are properly informed and consulted. The deacons are responsible for the making ready of a suitable place for baptism and for ensuring the provision of suitable dress for those ministering and receiving baptism. Suitable persons should be provided to assist the baptised person immediately following his immersion. The deacons are to see that all is done decently.

Rom. 6:3; Eph. 6:1, 2; 1 Cor. 12:13; Mark 16:15; Acts 8:35-39; Titus 2:3, 4; 1 Tim. 5:2; Acts 6:4; 1 Cor. 14:40.

The Place of Baptism

Any place is suitable which has adequate water and where confession of repentance and faith can be made. It would normally be in a public place before the christian congregation, and not done privately. Baptism will normally follow the ministry of the Word and is best administered in the context of public worship which provides for the proper teaching of all present. The minister may exhort the assembly, suitably giving the meaning of the ordinance and adding an exhortation to the candidate as to the consequence of his obedience to Christ's command.

Mat. 3:5-6; John 3:23; Acts 8:12, 13, 36; Mat. 28:19; Acts 2; Acts 8; Mat. 3:1-12; John 1:19-28.

The Method of Baptism

Some may find it appropriate to invite a simple confession of faith by the candidate, asking him such a question as, *Do you repent of your sins before God, and trust alone in the Lord Jesus Christ for salvation?* This would normally find adequate response in the simple affirmation *I do*. The minister will normally enter the water with the candidate, standing in a manner suitable for the latter's total immersion without danger of indecency. He will hold the candidate securely, inspiring confidence and making full use of the buoyancy of the water. He may address him, using such words as *My brother in Christ . . .* (then either his full name or first name) *. . . upon your profession of repentance towards God and faith in the Lord Jesus Christ I baptise you in the Name of the Father and of the Son and of the Holy Spirit. Amen.* The minister will then quickly but carefully immerse the candidate and set him back on his feet in a position suitable for leaving the water. Elder brethren and sisters can assist the candidate at this stage as well as in drying and re-dressing afterwards. The congregation may sing a verse of praise or a doxology, and the minister conclude the service with a Gospel exhortation or call to discipleship, as he is led.

Acts 8:38; Col. 2:12; Mat. 28:19; Acts 2:38, 39.

Pastoral After-care

Pastoral care should follow the baptism of all candidates, whatever their age, with the purpose of leading them into full fellowship of the local church, assisting them to take their place as christians in the world by continued instruction in the Word. There is a particular need for this after-care in the case of those who have not had the benefit of christian family life and instruction.

Eph. 4:5; 1 Cor. 12:13; 10:3, 4.

THE LORD'S SUPPER

The Meaning

The Lord's Supper is a memorial of the sufferings and death of the Lord Jesus Christ in the symbols of bread and wine, and an expression of the unity of the church as one body in Christ. The participants feed by faith on Christ crucified, and all the benefits of his death. By this means, faith is confirmed, hope is quickened and love awakened.

Mat. 26:26-28; Mark 14:22-24; Luke 22:15-20; Acts 2:42-46; 1 Cor. 10:16-17; 11:23-26.

The Participants

Those are the right persons to gather for the Lord's Supper who are in fellowship with the local church, and are come together to participate fully in its fellowship. A true humility, sometimes being expressed as *unworthy to come* is not to be confused with a lack of discernment and unspirituality which make a person altogether unworthy. Persons should not come to the Lord's Table who are under the excluding discipline of the church—heretics, those of unworthy motives holding anything unforgiven against another, or with known sin not repented of or other spiritual hindrances to a proper discernment of the essential oneness in Christ. Similarly, believers who deliberately refuse the instruction of the Word as given within the church by its elders, or who disobey the commandments of the Lord (such as baptism or to love one another) should not present themselves. Persons known to be unqualified, whose presence at the Lord's Table would occasion a breach of fellowship, should be requested to withdraw by the elders. If a person, having shared in the Lord's Supper is found subsequently to be an unworthy partaker to the hurt of the church, he should be dealt with as a disorderly person as Scripture directs (see page 44). Humble repentance, followed by a gracious obedience, would make such a person acceptable again and in this, pastoral care is most desirable and fruitful. Failure to respond graciously and offer submission to the Word of God taught, would in itself require the church to take stern action and this, in the case of hardened persistence, would lead to exclusion from the church. An unbaptised person, though a believer, who has been properly instructed in the scriptural truth of the ordinance of believer's baptism and who refuses to submit to the

82

Word, would come within this discipline of the church.

1 Cor. 11:27-34; 5:5, 11; Rom. 16:17; 2 Thess. 3:6, 14, 15.

The Frequency

This ordinance should be frequently administered within the fellowship of each gathered local church, because it is a sign of the common salvation and a remembrance of Christ's death and resurrection, according to His own command. When the church gathers freely and very frequently as in liberal contemporary societies, an over-frequent administration may take something of the true meaning from the ordinance. But in antagonistic societies such as that in which the early church was born, or in modern anti-christian states, a breaking of bread as often as the church is able to meet may be appropriate. It seems right to regulate the frequency of the ordinance, and a weekly or monthly interval may best suit our conditions. Adequate notice should be given to all the believers in each church fellowship so that all may properly prepare themselves to participate in the ordinance. The Lord's Supper must never be approached lightly or carelessly, nor should its administration be indifferently arranged in the church's programme or worship.

Acts 20:7; 1 Cor. 11:28.

The Occasion

Scripture does not lay down a rigid context for the ordinance in the church's gathering for worship, except that Paul says *when you come together to eat.* Since the coming together of the church is for prayer, worship and the ministry of the Word, it would appear that these elements of worship in fellowship should be associated with the administration. It is suitably placed in the context of church worship rather than in a gathering where a large admixture of unbelievers might be present. It may be observed when and wherever the local church is gathered as a disciplined assembly. This precludes its observation during occasions when christians are gathered in conventions, conferences, holiday parties, etc. The taking of the bread and wine of the Lord's supper to an invalid appears foreign to scripture, whereas the gathering of the church at the bedside for the supper is consistent.

1 Cor. 11:33.

Visiting Believers

A visitor remaining in the district and enjoying the fellowship of the church shall be deemed by this latter action to have voluntarily placed himself under its spiritual care and discipline. He shall be required to accept equally the privileges and responsibilities of such fellowship. Visiting believers in good standing in their own home fellowships, temporarily gathered with another local church, may participate in its fellowship including the Lord's Supper and other of its spiritual activities, provided that there is credible evidence of their being regenerate persons, and a willing submission to the discipline of the church for the period of their presence with it. An unwillingness to submit to the ministry of the Word and the allied discipline of the church shall cause such a person to be dealt with in the same manner as any other *member* of the fellowship.

Acts 20:7.

The Manner of the Ordinance

The deacons shall furnish the table suitably, with such convenient articles as shall enable the ordinance to be kept with reverence, including the provision of bread and wine (or, some would say, other common beverage). It is suitable, though not essential, for the table to be laid as for a meal, the bread presented suitably for ease of breaking by the minister, and the wine already poured from its bottle into a suitable vessel. The elders shall have appointed in advance a minister to lead the service, and should gather with him at the table. There may be suitable singing, the offering of prayer, and the exposition of scripture. A warning should be given against improper approach to the table, together with encouragement to needy and sensitive believers regarding the welcome inherent in the Lord's command so to gather. The minister may use suitable words of scripture such as 1 Cor. 11 : 23-27 at the distribution. He, or some other, should offer a prayer of thanksgiving for the bread, which symbolises the breaking of the Lord's body for his people. Then the bread shall be broken and distributed to the assembled church. The bread may conveniently be broken into small portions by the minister and distributed upon suitable plates by appointed persons. Similarly, the minister shall pour the wine into suitable cups for distribution to the gathered church. Thanksgiving being offered, the words of institution may then be repeated and the distribution made by appointed persons. Some churches use the *common cup* though sometimes a larger church may for convenience employ two or more. But where *individual cups* are used, the service should be the more carefully ordered to avoid any loss of true memorial in the service. The use of other than a common cup, though it be permissible in itself, may introduce an element foreign to the simplicity of the remembrance, and take away part of its highest intention. The *oneness* in the *communion* lies not in the overt act of all drinking but in the fact that all are identified with the Lord Jesus Christ. Whatever practice is adopted, it is essential that the church preserve inviolate the spiritual essence of this service. After all the communicants have participated, the minister may remind them of the *Grace of God in Jesus Christ* held forth in this ordinance, and exhort all present to walk worthy of it. This may be followed by prayer and the singing of a hymn or doxology before the members disperse or proceed to other ministries.

The Offering

In many churches an offering is taken for the needy. This should be so ordered as not to hinder the communion of the gathered church.

Remembering the Absent

A welcome may be extended to visitors or new members coming to the table for the first time. Similarly, special remembrance and prayer may be made on behalf of those prevented from attending by age or illness, and for any advised by the elders not to attend as a matter of discipline or pastoral care. This will best be done at an early point in the order of service.

Conclusion

Responsibility rests upon the elders of any local church to warn against improper participation, and to maintain the highest spiritual and scriptural standards of fellowship in every way. Restriction of admission to the ordinance is an integral part of overall pastoral care for the health of the fellowship in the whole of its life. Where a living church is under the discipline of the Word, and high standards of pastoral care prevail, the arbitrary use of regulations will become less necessary. A healthy, well-disciplined fellowship, sitting under the Word will need no other guide or scheme for dealing with the presence of visitors in the midst.

THE PRAYER MEETING

One of the essential marks of a believer is that he prays, and one of the distinguishing marks of a gospel church is that the believers meet regularly to seek the will of God, his cleansing and renewing, in prayer together. Those praying in this way ought to be in spiritual health, having no unconfessed sin or improper attitude towards their fellow-believers. All who are gathered should seek the filling of the Holy Spirit, so that they may know the liberty of the children of God in holy boldness and exultant joy. The scripture also makes it clear that in the exercise of prayer the headship of man in the church and family should not be usurped by the woman. If and when women pray they should respect the scriptural principle of submission.

THE CHURCH MEETING

Precedents in Scripture

Churches determine their policy at gatherings known as church meetings. Here the membership gathers to uphold and proclaim the government of the church by our Lord Jesus Christ. At a church meeting, a church seeks to discover God's will for itself by prayer and submission to God's Word, and also prays for power and perseverance to do that will. Such meetings should be held regularly, perhaps either monthly or quarterly.

Reasons for which the Church met in the New Testament

The following list indicates the variety of such purposes:—

Acts 1:15-26	The replacement of an apostle
2:1	Waiting on the Lord
6:2-6	Setting aside men for special administration
11:22	Providing for inter-church fellowship
13:1	The ministry of the Word
13:2, 3	The sending of missionaries
14:27	Rehearsing God's mighty acts
15:1-29	The defence and confirmation of the Gospel
15:30-31	Receiving communications from brethren
1 Cor. 5:1-5	The discipline of offenders
(also Mat. 18:15-20)	
1 Cor. 11:17-34	Observing the Lord's Supper
14:26	The exercise of spiritual gifts
2 Cor. 7:19	To deal with monetary gifts
Col. 4:16	The reading of the Word
(also 1 Thess. 5:27)	

The above passages indicate that the church meeting is warranted and required by scripture.

Purposes for Gathering

These scriptures also suggest a number of guidelines for the conduct of church meetings. It is evident that the whole church should be gathered, and all members should make every endeavour to be present. For convenience we may distinguish between meetings for *business* and those for *spiritual* matters, but there is no fundamental difference between them. Business meetings are also spiritual meetings. The spirit of prayer and worship should pervade them all. As the matters discussed have to do with eternal issues, it is good to remember the Lord's abiding promise that where his church is gathered in his name, he is in the midst. The whole church should be concerned in dealing with the defence of the truth, the ordering of worship, the appointment of elders and deacons, the sending out of missionaries, evangelistic problems and projects and the discipline of disorderly members. Routine business such as finance, the maintenance of buildings, etc., should be dealt with by the deacons without the need of referring details to the church for decisions. Nevertheless, reports of such matters should be given regularly so that all may be seen to be honestly conducted, not only before God but before men.

Mat. 18:19; Acts 13:3; 2 Cor. 8:21.

Procedure to be Adopted at Church Meetings

When the church meets to make decisions, the object is not primarily to discover the majority opinion, but rather to discover the mind of Christ. It may be a useful device to discover the opinion of the members by taking their votes for or against a recommendation, but it ought to be noted that the New Testament churches adopted no such procedure in making their decisions. There will be times when the majority vote must prevail over the minority, but divided opinion is often a signal that the matter should be referred back to the elders for further prayerful and biblical consideration. The ideal is that the mind of the Lord be revealed by the unanimity of his people. The most helpful procedure suggested by scripture for the handling of business is that matters brought to the church shall have been first considered by the elders. It is unwise for a proposal to come to the church that does not have their unanimous support. Each item brought before the church ought to be the subject of deliberate and specific prayer. Then, all the relevant facts should be set before the church together with the appropriate biblical evidence and requirements. The members may be expected to give willing consent to the guidance of their appointed leaders, except in some extreme matters of conscience. The elders are to be submissive to the Lord, the members to submit to the elders, and all to submit to each other in the fear of the Lord.

1 Thess. 5:12, 13; Heb. 13:17; Eph. 5:21.

The elders are responsible for ensuring that all meetings are conducted in an atmosphere of prayer, love and mutual trust. They must see that everything is done in an orderly and upright manner. Talkative members should be restrained, and those who are timid encouraged. There must be a place for the exercise of gifts and talents, each member contributing to the life of the whole fellowship. All are to strive to keep the unity of the Spirit in the bond of peace. If church members deliberately sought to stir each other up to love and good works, the church meeting would become a means of committing the church to action according to the will of God.

Eph. 4:3; Heb. 10:24, 25.

MAINTAINING CHURCH ORDER

Church discipline includes:

The Necessity for Maintaining Church Order. The need for each local church to discipline its life and order follows from three basic principles:

1. **The gathered church:** Ideally, the church is a fellowship of regenerate people and ought only to receive into its membership born-again believers.

The *gathered church* means a church made up not of those who once professed to be called out of the world to follow Christ, but of those who still do so. It follows that those who turn back on their profession, or who give other reason to the church to believe that they are not truly converted, must be removed from membership.

2. **The ordered church:** The church stands for the truth of the Gospel and for Christian morality. It exists to bear witness to both in the world and to further this end it has an ordered structure and fellowship. If a member violates its standards, action must be taken to restore its order, both for its own purity and for the sake of its public witness.

   Titus 2:1-5.

3. **The voluntary principle:** A person joins a church not under any coercion but by his own desire. In doing so, he takes upon himself both privileges and responsibilities. The responsibilities include making a full contribution to the life of the church and living a consistent christian life on the personal level. Since he has willingly consented to these principles, the church is right to act when they are violated.

   2 Cor. 8:5; Acts 2:41-44.

The New Testament yields abundant examples of churches maintaining their order in this way. They cover many different situations including offences against the peace and fellowship of the church, heresy, sin in a member's personal life, disputes between members and disputes between churches.

Mat. 18:15-20; Acts 15:1-33; Rom. 16:17; 1 Cor. 5:1, 2; 2 Cor. 13:1, 2; Gal. 6:1; 2 Thess. 3:6, 11, 12; 1 Tim. 1:20; 5:20; Titus 1:13; 3:8-10.

The Purpose in Maintaining Church Order

In maintaining its order, the church is acting in self-preservation. Its life is spiritual and sin can destroy it. If sin is tolerated in the midst, the whole life of the church suffers and the fellowship is marred.

1 Cor. 5:6; Rev. 2:14; 6:20.

Errors of belief and practice, if overlooked, deny the very message proclaimed by the church. A telling witness demands consistency. The church acts against sin within itself in order to preserve effective witness. Where the members know that the church will take action to preserve its order, they are discouraged from sin. This is heightened if they see instances of such discipline being carried out.

Titus 2:1-5; 1 Tim. 5:20.

The church is also acting for the highest good of the one who has sinned. It is giving proof that it takes a serious view of sin in the christian, but it is doing much more than this. The real aim is that the guilty person should be brought to repentance and restored to full fellowship in the church. All such action should be effected faithfully, but not harshly nor arrogantly. It must always be done in christian love and humility.

2 Tim. 2:24-26; Titus 1:13; 1 Cor. 5:5; Gal. 6:1; 2 Cor. 2:6-8; Rev. 3:19.

The Means of Maintaining Church Order

It is a vital necessity for the spiritual life of the church that only converted people are admitted into membership. The membership of any who give positive cause for doubt should be reconsidered, and those that actually give evidence that they are not converted should be removed from membership altogether. Such removal should never be done without ministering to the one concerned, and in love seeking to help him. The teaching ministry of the church must include detailed instruction in christian living and standards of behaviour, both on the personal level and within the corporate life of the fellowship. This includes not only the public preaching of the Word, but also the particular application to the individual in private, through pastoral care. Offences can be called *personal* when they concern a personal relationship where an injury has been done, or is thought to be done, by one member to another. They can be termed *general* when they concern error, heresy, morals, breaches of love, neglect of responsibility, or in any other way injure the cause of Christ.

Personal Offences: Christians are forbidden to go to law against their brethren. In case of wrongs, there are two courses of action. One is patiently to suffer the wrong done, and not to seek reparation. The other is to have the matter decided by a wise man in the church. Members who find themselves in a situation that cannot be resolved privately may ask the elders of the church to decide it. If the professed injury is proved, it may involve the wrong-doer in censure. In cases where a quarrel between members is disrupting the fellowship of the church, the elders should call for the dispute to be heard before them, and it may be necessary to rebuke both parties.

1 Cor. 6:1-7; Mat. 18:15-17.

General Offences: As in the case of personal offences, the first person to have knowledge of a general offence should make personal and private efforts to remedy the situation if this be possible. Failing this, he must notify the elders. Having thus obtained a formal knowledge of the matter, they will visit the brother concerned in the name of the Lord and of the church, to hear his explanations and intentions. They will go in a spirit of love and meekness, desiring to win the brother. If this first visit does not resolve the matter, it may be necessary to warn the offender of the error of his ways and to require him to come before the church. If, when this happens, the offender should disprove the charges made against him, or should he admit them and confess his wrong, making suitable acknowledgment and reparation, this should be deemed sufficient and the case dismissed. If the offender defies the authority of the church and refuses to appear before it, or if he cannot appear, the church will reach its decision prayerfully and justly and mercifully in the light of

92

all available evidence. But if all patient, deliberate and prayerful effort to reclaim the offender finally fails, excommunication must follow upon due admonition.

Titus 1:13; 1 Tim. 5:20; Titus 3:10; 2 Cor. 2:6-8.

The aim of excommunication is not only the church's purity but also the offender's good. It is reformative as well as punitive. The person excommunicated can be restored upon repentance. It is essential that all members are aware of the church's position in its control over them. They should be regularly reminded of this, and more important still, it should be ensured that new members fully understand this when they join the fellowship. It will avoid misunderstanding if pastoral exhortation and censure are specifically clarified to prospective members when joining the church. This activity of discipline must be constant and consistent, avoiding the sudden purge.

1 Tim. 1:20; 2 Thess. 3:15; 1 Cor. 5; Gal. 6:1; 1 Tim. 5:22 (see also vv. 20-21).

The Special Place of Elders and Deacons: The disciplinary ministry of the church is through the elders. They are responsible for teaching and encouraging the members, for the execution of church censures, and the pastoral care of the subjects of censure. There are several points of difference when the church has to deal with sin on the part of an elder or deacon.

Heb. 13:17; Acts 20:17, 28; 1 Pet. 5:1, 2; 1 Thess. 5:12; Gal. 6:1.

An accusation against an elder is more serious than one against other members. Elders are also more vulnerable than others to accusation, and their reputation must be protected. Consequently, such an accusation should be heard only in the presence of several witnesses so that every word may be established.

1 Tim. 5:19 f.

93

Officers accept great responsibilities, and if they fail to live up to these they render themselves liable to the censure of the church. Sins of office include failure to fulfil their duties, using their privileges for personal gain or selfish prestige, and instigating party spirit. Such a person should not continue to hold office. It may be advisable while an accusation against an office-bearer is being heard to suspend him from office until the matter is resolved.

1 Pet. 5:2, 3.

Dangers to Avoid in Discipline

Heresy Hunting: Those in the church who pry into the affairs of others, or are constantly on the look-out for sins and errors create an atmosphere which will be deadening to that brotherly love and trust which should characterise a christian fellowship.

Assuming the Accused Person Guilty: Christian love demands that we believe the best about a person until we are forced to conclude otherwise. The elders should examine an accusation before it is brought before the church to see if there be a case to answer. The charge must be solidly proved by two or three witnesses, and unless or until that is done, the member should be assumed innocent.

1 Cor. 13: 6, 7; 2 Cor. 13:1.

Errors in applying censure: Churches can make mistakes. It is possible to censure a member wrongly, or to fail to administer censure where it is due. It is important to rectify such mistakes with all possible speed. They may bring the gospel into disrepute outside the church, or impair the authority of all discipline within it. The aim of the censure is to edify both the wrong-doer and the church, but where it is wrongly applied, the effect will be nullified. For these reasons, a church guilty of any such miscarriage of justice should rejoice at having it pointed out.

1 Cor 5:1, 2, 11.

INTER-CHURCH RELATIONS

Consideration of relations between churches should always be based on a clear understanding of the independence of each local church. A sufficiency in the Lord makes the local church free from external authority in all matters of doctrine and discipline, and adequate for the demands of Christ's missionary commission. Yet this independency should not be interpreted in terms of isolation. Although independent of external authorities, churches are bound by a spiritual and biblical necessity to give practical expression to their love to one another and their unity in Christ. The *Body of Christ* is seen not only in the local church but also in the voluntary fellowship of independent churches. There are three particular areas of such fellowship:—

1. **Co-operation.** Those who are strong ought to help bear the burden of the weak in the support of missionaries sent out from among them. Consultation between churches about opportunities and policies relating to missionary enterprise is desirable.

2. **Consultation.** In days of general confusion and slackness, it is right for churches to seek agreement about doctrines, and about the application of discipline, so that like-minded local churches can honour the disciplinary actions of one another. Speaking the truth in love, churches that are strong in the faith ought to seek to win back those churches that are in danger of departing from it and thus causing damage to the unity and witness of all.

3. **Co-ordination.** In matters of works of charity those who are strong should bear the burdens of others in this country and overseas. Churches must care for one another both in spiritual and in material matters.

The basis of inter-church fellowship is adherence to sound doctrine, and the experience of the power of the Holy Spirit. An orthodox statement of doctrine is inadequate without a living conviction and experience. Such fellowship must honour the independence of the local church, being enjoyed voluntarily under the constraint of the Holy Spirit through the Word. Furthermore, it is not primarily organisational, and any institution associated with it should be for certain specific and limited objectives, and not necessarily a permanent structure. These characteristics of honouring sound doctrine and local church independency, and of a spiritual rather than institutional unity are not found in the ecumenical movement as reflected in the *British Council of Churches* or the *World Council of Churches*.

In working out the practical implications of these principles it must be conceded that there are degrees of fellowship. While all true gospel churches should be seen to be at one, it is clear that those who have most in common will be drawn most closely together in practice. There ought to be no hindrance to inter-church fellowship between all who hold to the reformed and baptist teaching of scripture, along with the principle of restricted communion. This is recognised and realised in ministerial fraternals, local associations, fellowship groups and in the Strict Baptist Mission. In such settings and in the bonds of christian love, churches may receive and give advice to one another, and pastors and people assist and encourage each other in mutual joy and sympathy. The degree of fellowship will be limited when Arminian doctrine and methods of evangelism intrude, along with ecumenical involvements and non-baptist teaching. Great care is needed in working out a balance between the ideals, as seen in the New Testament, and dangerous and compromising involvements in our own day. Yet at no time should the differences between essentially evangelical churches become a matter of unseemly conflict.

Eph. 1:19; 2 Cor. 8 and 9; Acts 15:1 through to 16:5; Gal. 1:8; 2 John 9-11; 1 Thess. 2:14.

Part 3   WITNESS

EVANGELISM—LOCAL AND GLOBAL

Evangelism is the activity of the people of God in bringing the message of the gospel to those who have not heard it, or do not believe it. It includes all the work of making known the gospel, whether at home or abroad. The Lord Jesus Christ commanded his apostles to evangelise. The command is to go to every race, tribe or group of people in the world and is operative until his coming again. We live in an age when the most remote areas of the world are being opened up, and the world's population is greater than ever before. The command to evangelise is more relevant than ever. For the people of God, this command is at once their particular privilege and their responsibility alone—none other will do it!

> Mat. 18:20; Mark 16:15; Luke 24:47; Acts 1:8; Isa. 49:6; Rom. 10:14, 15.

The Importance of Doctrine

The theology we hold will determine our approach and method in evangelism. Biblical evangelism must be rooted in biblical doctrine, drawing from it both its authority and its motive power. The evangelist must understand the doctrines of *Total Depravity* and *Regeneration*. Man in his sin is not free to come to God by his own will, but must be born again by the sovereign work of the Holy Spirit. Gospel preaching must declare the whole counsel of God, and proclaim him as both holy and righteous, as creator and judge. The preaching of the law of God with its implications for all men should be accompanied by the preaching of the grace of God, through the substitutionary sacrifice of our Lord Jesus Christ. The faithful preacher will not fail to warn his hearers of everlasting punishment, nor to hold out the promise of everlasting life to all those who believe.

97

The Godly Life of the Church

One of the most vital factors in evangelism is the reflection of the life and character of the Lord Jesus Christ in the local church. Love, joy, unity, holiness and good works are essential to evangelistic testimony. Enquirers after truth cannot but be encouraged where these are consistently present.

Responsibility for Organisation

Besides maintaining its own life and vitality, every local church has the responsibility (in proportion to the numbers and gifts that God has given to them) of spreading the gospel to every person in their neighbourhood. They must also contribute in a realistic way to the evangelisation of other areas of the world. This demands some measure of organisation, and the elders of each church are responsible to guide in this matter.

Methods

Every local church must submit itself to the guidance of the Holy Spirit within its own particular circumstances. The following guide-lines do not necessarily apply to every church.

Services of the Lord's Day: The forthright preaching of the gospel, supported by the faithful attendance and joyful participation of the church members is honoured by a gracious God. Those members who feel ungifted for any other means of evangelism may play a part here.

Personal Confrontation: Every believer is required to be ready to give a reason for the hope that is in him to any who may enquire. Beyond this, some are gifted with the ability to make direct approaches to individual men and women with the gospel. Such approaches may result from contact in the daily routine of life, or from encounters at the auxiliary meetings of a christian fellowship (such as women's meetings, youth meetings, home study groups, etc.) or from the systematic visitation of homes in the area.

Christian Literature: Tracts and booklets may be used in widespread distribution, but great care should be taken that their contents are of a high standard, and thoroughly scriptural. Nor should it be forgotten that one personal conversation is normally of far greater value than the giving out of vast quantities of impersonal literature.

Working Together: It is physically impossible for any one church to be involved in every type of evangelistic work, and it will therefore be found profitable to work with other churches to further the Lord's work at home and abroad. The *Strict Baptist Mission* is a case in point. In this way the gospel has been preached world-wide by men and women who have been supported by the churches in personal evangelism, literature production and radio ministry.

Special Services: Some men are especially gifted by God as able evangelistic preachers. Their ministries should be shared among the churches either in chapels or in the open air. But this must never be regarded as a substitute for consistent effort by the whole church at all times.

Aids to Evangelism: Hospitality and the generous use of the christian home are important factors in evangelism and should be given every possible encouragement. Advertising media can also be profitably used to bring the local church to the attention of the community.

The Prayer Meeting: Here, the responsibility of outreach should be laid before the Lord. The various possibilities should be considered in the light of the gifts which the Lord has given to the church. It is seriously to be questioned whether any person should be permitted to engage in the church's outreach who does not regularly attend one of the prayer meetings.

Assured Results: Not all who hear the gospel proclaimed will be saved, but believers evangelise with the sure knowledge that, whatever their local circumstances, God's cause will finally triumph.

Psa. 22:27; Dan. 2:31-35; Isa. 55:11; Ezek. 33:8, 9; 1 Cor. 15:27, 28, 58; Rev. 7:9.

AUXILIARY OUTREACH

Young People's Work

Parental Responsibility: Responsibility rests upon parents to train up their children in the ways of God, and this should include instruction in the scriptures with a clear presentation of the gospel. No community or church provision for religious education, however Bible-orientated it may be, can relieve christian parents of this obligation. The family is an important factor in the growth and stability of a church because the character of the families comprising each fellowship will reflect its spiritual calibre. Children must learn the fifth commandment and its implications. They must learn obedience. They are to be taught to obey because God has commanded it, and such obedience should be given willingly, as honour afforded to the parent, and not grudgingly. The Bible teaches the parents to use reproof and punishment, tempered with wisdom and mercy. Children ought not to be exasperated, discouraged or subjected to physical cruelty. Children should be brought up in an atmosphere where all problems are dealt with in the context of scripture. All such teaching must be in the context of an acknowledgement of God as creator and man as his creature.

Eph. 6:1-3; Prov. 13:24; 19:18; 29:15-17; Eph. 6:4.

Church's Responsibility: The church may do well to strengthen the hands of the membership and repair any deficiencies in parental instruction by means of special classes either on Sundays or other days. Such classes will be taught by church members appointed for their spiritual qualities as well as natural teaching gifts, because the teaching of God's

100

Word is by practice as much as by precept. The Bible will be the text book, and will be taught out of a firm conviction of its divine authority as God's Word, its capability to make the sinner wise unto salvation and fully equip the believer for all that God requires of him in this life.

Sunday Schools: Sunday Schools were first introduced as a means of evangelism among children of unbelievers or unconcerned nominal christians. The needs of all children are the same. In some situations the absence of family instruction may make it neither practical nor wise for the church to seek to fulfil its obligations to its own families alongside the children from pagan backgrounds, who lack all teaching and example. The reaching and gathering in of children from unevangelised homes is a most proper and rewarding means of gospel ministry. The same high standards must be maintained in the appointment of teachers and in the teaching itself. Indeed, particular care should be taken because these children are not being instructed in christian truth at home.

Bible Classes: Traditionally, older children are given special instruction in groups appropriate to their ages, often called Bible classes. Outreach work may be done on weekdays, perhaps utilising different methods but with the same end in view namely conversion and training in the Word of God.

Youth Meetings: Young people's activities with clear spiritual principles are to be commended to meet the needs of the families of christians. The social need for recreation may be used as a means of reaching pagan society with the gospel. But there can be a danger in confusing the social needs of the families of christian parents with those of others. Care must be taken to avoid worldliness and the lowered standards of pagan society, for the encroachment of these influences would destroy the spiritual ministry of the church, whether on its own premises or elsewhere. Generally speaking, social welfare work is better undertaken under the administration of the local education and health authorities where christians can fulfil their duties to the community as good citizens and also bear an effective christian influence and testimony to the gospel.

Teaching Aids: The church's use of *teaching systems* in its Sunday School or classes demands the exercise of constant care. Any system employed should be closely aligned to the faith and order of the church. It should be realised what is involved in effective teaching and learning. Scripture reveals timeless principles—for example, direct question-and-answer catechism, and memorisation of the scripture. It is important that new means to disseminate facts and ideas be used as efficiently as possible, provided that the methods themselves do not detract from the gospel.

Exod. 13:8; Deut. 6:7 and 20-25; Josh. 12:26-28.

Women's Fellowships

Whilst no case can be made for fragmenting the worship or fellowship of the church on grounds of age or sex, yet there is reason for using the ease with which women are gathered together as a special opportunity for evangelism. Many churches find themselves able to convene regular gatherings of unconverted women and to present the gospel to them. All such outreach should be under the direct control of the church and accountable to it. All the programming should be consistent with the church's standing and only speakers used able to meet this requirement.

Acts 16:13; 17:4.

Home Study Groups

The unconverted are frequently reached by the discreet use of meetings held in the homes of members where the Word of God can be expounded in surroundings acceptable to the community at large. Such ministry should be regulated carefully by the pastoral leadership of the church and the inexperienced or untaught should not engage in regular teaching. Unwise laxity in this can lead to unbalanced emphases in teaching and formation of 'house-churches' of a divisive character calculated to breach rather than further fellowship.

Acts 16:31, 32; 20:20, 21; 1 Cor. 1:10-18.

Utilisation of Places of Worship and Halls

Christian places of worship are not set apart in any sacramental way as were the tabernacle and temples of Israel. The people of God themselves constitute the *Temple of God.* The provision of specialised buildings is a convenience but not a necessity. Though they cannot be *desecrated* yet thoughtless usage can hinder the gospel. The church's evangelistic outreach and its fulfilment of christian concern towards the community may justify use for such purposes as *nursery schools, playgroups, charitable care of the aged and handicapped, youth groups, clubs, coffee-mornings, wedding receptions, etc.,* as well as the gathering of the church socially. All such use may be lawful yet be deemed not expedient in a local situation. Careful discrimination ought to be exercised lest the testimony of the church of God's holy people be damaged by any indiscretion. Let all be done to the glory of God and all else be excluded.

1 Cor. 3:16, 17; Eph. 2:19-22; 1 Cor. 11:20-22; 6:12; 10:23; 1 Pet. 1:13-16; 1 Cor. 10:31.

THE SOCIAL CONCERN OF THE CHURCHES

The churches have a responsibility to awaken christians to practical social concern. Believers are to separate themselves from ungodliness, but not to isolate themselves from society. They are to be the light of the world, working out their faith as responsible citizens.

John 17:15; 1 Cor. 5:10; Mat. 5:16.

The witness of the churches and of individual christians to the gospel is to be accompanied by *good works.* The love of Christ will constrain his people to share the burden of human need, giving hospitality, visiting the lonely and sad, and showing compassion to the wayward. Christ's disciples are to be good neighbours.

Mat. 5:16; Titus 2:14; Mat. 25:35-46; 22:36-40; Mark 1:41; 6:34; 8:1; Gal. 6:10; James 1:26, 27.

Even in a *Welfare State* christians ought not to forsake this concern by leaving all such care to *the authorities* because, apart from christian motivation, social welfare can become mechanical and dehumanised. Christians should be encouraged, where suitable, to enter the professional aspects of social service, medical care, child welfare, mental health work, etc., whilst non-professional and voluntary work in hospitals, prisons, charities, etc., can provide opportunities for others. The same principle applies to the moral needs of society. Christians are to be the salt of the earth. This means that, apart from any specific endeavour, their very way of life should hinder the spread of corruption. Our Lord mixed with *publicans and sinners.* He did not take part in their sin but rather confronted them with his compassionate Holiness. The preaching of the gospel itself ought to result in the abandonment of evil practices. The *Law of God* is held before men as his just requirements and as the only true basis for a healthy society. Since the civil authorities are responsible to God for their conduct of national affairs, believers are to bring biblical principles to bear on social and moral problems, and apply them as far as possible. These principles include the extent and limit of the state's authority, the citizen's duty to the state, the questions of anarchy and civil disobedience, and matters of education, the punishment of crime, divorce, abortion, property, work and wages, etc. Christians who are magistrates, politicians, trade union officials or members of professional associations have God-given opportunities to exert a healthy influence on society as a whole.

Mat. 5:13; Acts 19:19; Rom. 13.

GENERAL CONCLUSION

It is the duty of the churches to examine themselves in the light of the scriptures. Reformation with a view to conformity to biblical requirements ought to be a continuing process rather than an occasional upheaval. This duty ought to be carried out with much prayer and humbling before God. It should be preceded by adequate searching of the Word and instruction of the people. Zeal and godly determination will be tempered with gentleness and patience. The Lord will honour diligent reformation in the churches. Without obedience to the Lord we have no right to look for his favour. Besides necessary adjustment of church life to scripture there is the great need of the outpouring of the Holy Spirit. Humble obedience ought to be accompanied by an earnest believing plea for God to *rend the heavens and come down.*

2 Cor. 7:10, 11; Rev. 2:5; 3:19, 20; Isa. 64:1, 2.

Appendix

Grace Baptist Assembly

Baptist churches committed to the doctrines of grace have much in common. They share similar interests, concerns and responsibilities. Although each particular church is given everything necessary fully to constitute it a church by its Head, the Lord Jesus Christ, it will rejoice to acknowledge the existence of other churches. It will seek, out of a trust and love founded on a common confession of faith and order, to commit itself to mutual encouragement and care between the churches.

Grace Baptist Assembly is one expression of such fellowship.

The first Assembly was held in May 1980 following the voluntary winding up of two similar assemblies. The Strict Baptist Assembly had provided fellowship for churches since 1964 and the Assembly of baptised churches holding the doctrines of grace since 1976. In both of these there had come the conviction that it was desirable that one Assembly should provide the fellowship sought, particularly as many churches were involved in both assemblies.

PURPOSE

The object of Grace Baptist Assembly is to provide a fellowship in which churches of common faith may find mutual encouragement and counsel. It provides opportunities for sharing information and for consultation on a national level on issues of concern to the churches. It provides opportunities of co-operative endeavour especially in missionary and evangelistic work, publication of literature, social concern and theological education.

STATEMENT OF FAITH

The doctrinal standards of the Assembly are the 'Old London' Confession of Faith of 1689 and 'We Believe', the Strict Baptist Affirmation of Faith (second edition 1973).

ATTENDANCE

Churches attending the Assembly give prior notice of their agreement with one of the confessions and confirmation of their baptised membership. In this they recognise the other churches making the same statements.

Each church also makes contributions towards the expenses incurred in the Assembly's arrangements.

The Assembly exists only as long as it is sitting and consequently each church affirms its commitment as above for each Assembly that is held.

Churches are represented at the Assembly by men they have appointed for this purpose. These are usually pastors, elders or deacons, although other members may be appointed.

Provision is made for churches to make a continuing commitment to the other churches in the Assembly when circumstances make it impossible for them to send any members to attend.

Observers are welcome to the Assembly. As observers they do not have the right of participation. Observers may be appointed by churches which cannot subscribe fully to the basis of the Assembly. They may also be individuals whose churches do not attend the Assembly.

BUSINESS OF ASSEMBLY

The Assembly meets as and when necessary and normally the meetings are held in London. There is no essential commitment to an annual assembly.

All assembling churches receive written notice of the time,

place and purpose of an Assembly or of other convened meetings.

The Assembly encourages all definite efforts to further its purposes primarily through the churches themselves and also through agencies which are answerable to the churches.

COMMITTEE

A committee attends to arrangements for the Assembly and is responsible to it for the implementation of its decisions and the answering of questions raised.

AUTHORITY

Church authority rests in the local church. All co-operation in or contribution to Assembly endeavours by a local church is voluntary and not imposed.

The assembly may not interfere in the affairs of the local churches. When requested by a church, the Assembly may express opinions and offer advice, but it has no power to enforce its judgement. Each church will determine whether such judgements are in accordance with the Scripture.

RELATIONS WITH OTHER BODIES

The churches in the Assembly humbly recognise that there are many who believe in Jesus Christ according to the Scriptures and who are not able to subscribe to the basis of the Assembly. Every church and minister is free to encourage and participate in expressions of the oneness of all christians in their localities.

The churches in the Assembly also seek fellowship with those outside the United Kingdom.

NEW CHURCHES IN ASSEMBLY.

The churches in the Assembly welcome other churches into their fellowship. Details of future Assemblies may be obtained from the secretary at:

**139 Grosvenor Avenue,
London N5 2NH**